新编研究生
英语读写译教程

主　编◎胡　芳　冷雪飞
副主编◎张　倩　陈　玲
编　者◎黄海泉　陈　彧　胡忠青
　　　　宋小琴　石　诗　王　莉
　　　　周　韵

English for
Postgraduates

Reading, Writing & Translating

清华大学出版社
北京

内 容 简 介

本教材由纸质教材和线上练习资源两部分组成，共 8 个单元。纸质教材每单元设有阅读、写作和翻译三个模块。阅读模块按照大学科方向，围绕当前社会经济和科技发展热点话题选材，主题内容涵盖芯片、智能制造、智能服装、新能源、按需服务、3D 生物打印、绿色节能建筑和衍生设计。教材基于阅读技能和主题拓展双线编排，同时融入思政元素和人文思考。写作模块兼顾普适性和差异性，侧重学术英语写作的共性体裁特点。翻译模块在内容设置上与写作密切关联，通过大量实例展示，帮助学生熟悉常用功能句型，掌握翻译技巧。

线上练习资源与纸质教材相互补充，主要提供与主题阅读、学术写作和翻译相关的练习，学生可登录 www.tsinghuaelt.com 进行拓展学习。

版权所有，侵权必究。举报：010-62782989，beiqinquan@tup.tsinghua.edu.cn。

图书在版编目（CIP）数据

新编研究生英语读写译教程 / 胡芳，冷雪飞主编. —北京：清华大学出版社，2024.2
（2025.2 重印）
ISBN 978-7-302-65657-9

Ⅰ.①新…　Ⅱ.①胡…　②冷…　Ⅲ.①英语—阅读教学—研究生—教材　②英语—写作—研究生—教材　③英语—翻译—研究生—教材　Ⅳ.① H319.39

中国国家版本馆 CIP 数据核字（2024）第 036285 号

责任编辑：曹诗悦
封面设计：李伯骥
责任校对：王荣静
责任印制：杨　艳

出版发行：清华大学出版社
　　网　　址：https://www.tup.com.cn, https://www.wqxuetang.com
　　地　　址：北京清华大学学研大厦 A 座　　邮　编：100084
　　社 总 机：010-83470000　　邮　购：010-62786544
　　投稿与读者服务：010-62776969, c-service@tup.tsinghua.edu.cn
　　质量反馈：010-62772015, zhiliang@tup.tsinghua.edu.cn
印 装 者：涿州市般润文化传播有限公司
经　　销：全国新华书店
开　　本：185mm×260mm　　印　张：11.5　　字　数：235 千字
版　　次：2024 年 3 月第 1 版　　印　次：2025 年 2 月第 2 次印刷
定　　价：48.00 元

产品编号：099401-01

前　言

《新编研究生英语读写译教程》面向普通高校非英语专业研究生编写，结合《非英语专业学位研究生英语教学大纲》要求和普通高校研究生英语教学特点进行设计，旨在巩固和提升研究生通用英语能力，加强其学术英语阅读、写作与翻译能力，为专业学习和学术研究打好语言基础。

本教材共 8 个单元，每单元设有阅读、写作和翻译三个模块。阅读模块按照大学科方向，围绕当前社会经济和科技发展热点话题选材，主题内容涵盖芯片、智能制造、智能服装、新能源、按需服务、3D 生物打印、绿色节能建筑和衍生设计。教材基于阅读技能和主题拓展双线编排阅读模块内容。"阅读技巧"（Reading Skills）与"课文理解"（Understanding the Text）练习充分结合，引导学生通过快读、略读、联想和推理等多种阅读策略，全方位把握文章要点，深入了解阅读本质。依托阅读文章主题，设置"主题拓展"（Theme Exploration）和"真实项目展示"（Real-Life Project），同时融入思政元素和人文思考内容，引领研究生从低阶的识记、理解走向更高阶的分析、评价和创造。

教材的写作和翻译模块契合研究生阶段英语学习的目标要求，侧重学术英语写作和翻译。考虑到教材的使用对象可能来自不同学科方向，因此写作模块在内容的编排上兼顾普适性和差异性，侧重学术英语写作的共性特点，选取典型范例讲解英语学术语篇的文体特点、论文主要结构要素、学术规范等，同时在练习设置上又充分考虑不同学科方向的可操作性。翻译模块在内容设置上与写作密切关联，通过大量实例展示，帮助学生熟悉常用功能句型，掌握翻译技巧。

本教材附配线上练习资源。线上练习资源主要为与主题阅读、学术写作和翻译相关的拓展练习，以补充纸质教材内容，充分赋能教师混合式教学实践。

本教材供一学期使用，每单元学习任务建议用 5～6 课时完成。教材内容相对丰富，教师可结合研究生英语教学具体情况灵活取舍。

由于编者水平有限，错漏之处在所难免，敬请广大读者批评指正。

编者
2024 年 1 月

Contents

Unit 1 Smart World, Better World **1**
    Reading: Despite Chip Shortage, Chip Innovation Is Booming 2
    Writing: Introduction to Academic Writing 11
    Translating: 学术英语翻译概述 16

Unit 2 Living with AI **23**
    Reading: The Move from Old-School Manufacturing to Smart
              Manufacturing 24
    Writing: Avoiding Plagiarism 32
    Translating: 术语翻译和词性转换 38

Unit 3 Advanced Materials, Advanced Life **45**
    Reading: What Is Smart Clothing Technology and How Does It Work? ... 46
    Writing: Title, Affiliation, and Acknowledgements 55
    Translating: 学术论文标题翻译 59

Unit 4 New Energy, New Future **63**
    Reading: Technology: Powering the Future of Energy 64
    Writing: Abstract and Keywords 74
    Translating: 学术论文摘要翻译 79

Unit 5 The Future Is Now **85**
    Reading: Generative Design Proves That "The Future Is Now"
              for Engineers 86
    Writing: Introduction 94
    Translating: 学术论文引言翻译 99

Unit 6　On-Demand Economy 105

Reading: Eight Service Industries That Drive the On-Demand Economy ... 106
Writing: Literature Review 115
Translating: 被动句和定语从句翻译 120

Unit 7　Gene Editing: Hope or Disaster? 127

Reading: The Future of Medicine: 3D Printers Can Create Human Body Parts 128
Writing: Methods 138
Translating: 学术论文研究方法翻译 142

Unit 8　Architecture for the Renewable World 147

Reading: Daylighting: Here's Why Natural Light Is the Greatest Tool of Modern Architecture 148
Writing: Results and Discussion 156
Translating: 学术论文研究结果和讨论翻译 160

Bibliography 167

Unit 1

Smart World, Better World

Part I
Reading

Despite Chip Shortage, Chip Innovation Is Booming

Don Clark

① A global shortage of semiconductors has *cast* a cloud over the plans of carmakers and other companies. But there's a *silver lining* for Silicon Valley executives like Aart de Geus.

② He is chairman and co-chief executive of Synopsys, the biggest supplier of software that engineers use to design chips. That position gives Mr. de Geus an intimate perspective on a 60-year-old industry that until recently was showing its age.

③ Everyone now seems to want his opinion, as shown by the dozens of emails, calls and comments he received after addressing a recent online gathering for customers. Synopsys says people *tuned in* from 408 companies—more than double the number for an *in-person event* last held in 2019—and many weren't conventional chip makers.

④ They came from cloud services, consumer electronics companies, defense contractors, auto component providers, U.S. government agencies, universities, two Bitcoin mining companies and a furniture maker. Their *overriding* question is: How do you develop chips more quickly?

⑤ Even as a chip shortage is causing trouble for all sorts of industries, the semiconductor field is entering a surprising new era of creativity, from industry giants to innovative *start-ups* seeing a *spike* in funding from *venture capitalists* that traditionally avoided chip makers.

⑥ Taiwan Semiconductor Manufacturing Company and Samsung Electronics, for example, have managed the increasingly difficult *feat* of packing more transistors on each slice of silicon. IBM on Thursday announced another leap in **miniaturization**, a sign of continued U.S. **prowess** in the technology race.

⑦ Perhaps most striking, what was a **trickle** of new chip companies is now approaching a flood. **Equity** investors for years viewed semiconductor companies as too costly to set up, but in 2020 **plowed** more than $12 billion **into** 407 chip-related companies, according to CB Insights.

⑧ Though a tiny fraction of all venture capital investments, that was more than double what the industry received in 2019 and eight times the total for 2016. Synopsys is tracking more than 200 start-ups designing chips for artificial intelligence, the ultrahot technology powering everything from smart speakers to self-driving cars.

⑨ Cerebras, a start-up that sells massive artificial-intelligence processors that **span** an entire silicon **wafer**, for example, has attracted more than $475 million. Groq, a start-up whose chief executive previously helped design an artificial-intelligence chip for Google, has raised $367 million.

⑩ "It's a bloody miracle," said Jim Keller, a **veteran** chip designer whose résumé includes stints at Apple, Tesla, and Intel and who now works at the AI chip start-up Tenstorrent. "Ten years ago you couldn't do a hardware start-up."

⑪ The trends are not necessarily good news for chip customers, at least for the short term. Scarce supplies of many chips have manufacturers **scrambling** to increase production, and are adding to worries in Washington about reliance on foreign suppliers. Extra demand could extend the shortages, which are already expected to last into 2022.

⑫ High demand was evident in earnings for chip companies last quarter, which ended in March. Revenue grew 27 percent, for example, at NXP Semiconductors, a big maker of auto, communications, and industrial chips, even though it temporarily closed two Texas factories because of a **cold snap**.

⑬ The industry has historically been notorious for **booms and busts**, usually driven by purchasing swings for particular products like PCs and smartphones. Global chip revenue **slumped** 12 percent in 2019 before bouncing back with 10 percent growth last year, according to estimates from Gartner, a research firm.

⑭ But there is widening optimism that the cycles should moderate because chips are now used in so many things. Philip Gallagher, chief executive of the big electronics distributor Avnet, cited examples like sensors to track dairy cows, the flow of beer taps and utility pipes, and the temperature of produce. And the number of chips in mainstay products like cars and smartphones keeps rising, he and other executives say.

⑮ "This is a lasting growth cycle, not a short spike," said Kurt Sievers, NXP's chief executive.

⑯ A longtime industry watcher, Handel Jones, who heads the consultancy International Business Strategies, sees total chip revenues rising steadily to $1.2 trillion by 2030 from roughly $500 billion this year.

⑰ That growth could arrive just as the industry fundamentally changes. More companies are concluding that software running on standard Intel-style microprocessors is not the best solution for all problems. For that reason, companies like Cisco Systems and Hewlett Packard Enterprise have long designed specialty chips for products such as networking gear.

⑱ Giants like Apple, Amazon, and Google more recently have gotten into the act. Google's YouTube unit recently disclosed its first internally developed chip to speed video encoding. And Volkswagen even said last week that it would develop its own processor to manage autonomous driving.

⑲ Chip design teams are no longer working just for traditional chip companies, said Pierre Lamond, a 90-year-old venture capitalist who joined the chip industry in 1957. "They are breaking new ground in many respects," he said.

⑳ Chip design software gained popularity in the 1980s to streamline tasks that engineers once carried out with pencils and drafting tables, painstakingly drawing clusters of transistors and other components on chips. The software tools have continually evolved; some carmakers, for example, use Synopsys-powered simulations of how future chips will work to write software for them in advance, Mr. de Geus said.

㉑ Synopsys, which he co-founded in 1986, has grown steadily, partly by *acquisitions*, to a valuation of $36 billion.

㉒ Mr. de Geus said new growth was coming from what seemed like a problem: a slowdown in Moore's Law, industry shorthand for the *perennial* race to shrink chip circuitry so chips do more with less silicon. In response, he said, some companies are using Synopsys tools to design entire systems and bundles of smaller chips that work like a single processor.

㉓ During his recent speech to users, Mr. de Geus demonstrated how artificial-intelligence enhancements could allow Synopsys tools to automatically decide how best to situate and connect blocks of *circuitry* on a chip. A system managed by a single engineer did the work two to five times faster than a team of designers, Mr. de Geus said, while its design used up to 13 percent less energy.

㉔ "The ability to use AI to design AI chips, that is the ultimate cool," he said. "There you meet science fiction."

→ Words and Expressions

cast *vt.* to make light, a shadow, etc. appear in a particular place 投射（光、影子等）

silver lining a consoling or hopeful prospect in a sad or unpleasant situation（不幸或失望中的）一线希望

tune in to regulate (a radio or television set) in order to receive a certain station or program 收听；收看；调谐

in-person event 面对面活动

overriding *adj.* more important than anything else in a particular situation 最重要的；首要的；凌驾一切的

start-up *n.* a company that is just beginning to operate, especially an Internet company 刚成立的公司，新企业（尤指互联网公司）

spike *n.* a sudden large increase in something 猛增；急升

venture capitalist a speculator who makes money available for innovative projects (especially in high technology) 风险投资家，创业投资家

feat *n.* an action or a piece of work that needs skill, strength or courage 技艺；功绩

miniaturization *n.* the act of making on a greatly reduced scale 小型化，微型化

prowess *n.* a superior skill that you can learn by study and practice and observation 超凡的技术

trickle *n.* flowing in drops; the formation and falling of drops of liquid 滴，淌；细流

equity *n.* the value of a company's shares; the value of a property after all charges and debts have been paid（公司的）股本；资产净值

plow...into to invest; to buy property, shares in a company, etc. in the hope of making a profit 投资

span *vt.* to include a large area or a lot of things 包括（广大地区）；涵盖（多项内容）

wafer *n.* a thin slice of semiconductor (as silicon) used as a base for an electronic component or circuit 晶片

veteran *adj.* rendered competent through trial and experience 老练的，经验丰富的

scramble *vt.* to manage to achieve something with difficulty, or in a hurry, without much control 艰难/仓促地完成某事

cold snap a sudden short period of very cold weather 寒流，寒潮

booms and busts alternate periods of high and low levels of economic activity in the business cycle 繁荣与萧条；商业兴衰

slump *vi.* to fall in price, value, number, etc. suddenly and by a large amount（价格、价值、数量等）骤降，猛跌，锐减

acquisition *n.* a company, piece of land, etc. bought by somebody, especially another company; the act of buying it 收购的公司；购置的产业；购置；收购

perennial *adj.* continuing for a very long time; happening again and again 长久的；持续的；反复出现的

circuitry *n.* a system of electrical circuits or the equipment that forms this 电路系统；电路；电路装置

➔ Notes

1. **Synopsys** 美国新思科技公司
   为全球集成电路设计提供电子设计自动化（EDA）软件工具的主导企业，成立于 1986 年，总部位于美国加利福尼亚州山景城。该企业为全球电子市场提供技术先进的 IC 设计与验证平台，致力于复杂的芯片级系统（SoC）的开发。

2. **Bitcoin mining** 比特币挖矿
   比特币挖矿是获得比特币的一种方法。比特币是一种由开源的 P2P 软件产生的网络虚拟货币，要获得比特币，就必须去解复杂的算法。人们把比特币称为"数字黄金"，把寻找正确数字的过程称为挖矿。

3. **Taiwan Semiconductor Manufacturing Company (TSMC)** 台湾积体电路制造股份有限公司（台积电）

   台积电成立于1987年，是全球第一家专业积体电路制造服务企业，总部与主要工厂位于中国台湾的新竹市科学园区。

4. **Samsung Electronics** 三星电子

   三星集团旗下的子公司，韩国最大的消费电子产品及电子组件制造商，也是全球最大的信息技术公司。目前三星电子的主要经营项目包括半导体、行动通讯、数位影像、电信系统、IT解决方案及数字应用。

5. **CB Insights**

   CB (Chubby Brain) Insights是全球领先的科技市场数据平台，2008年成立于纽约。通过数据和智能算法，CB Insights为私募股权、风投、媒体、跨国及创业公司提供完整的技术及市场解决方案，并定期发布数据报告及行业榜单。

6. **NXP Semiconductors** 恩智浦半导体公司

   该公司前身为荷兰飞利浦公司的半导体事业部，2006年从飞利浦公司脱离出来。2015年，恩智浦收购飞思卡尔半导体，成为全球最大的非存储类半导体公司之一，为安全识别、汽车和数字网络领域提供半导体。

7. **Avnet** 安富利集团

   全球最大的电子元件、计算机产品和嵌入技术分销商之一，总部位于美国亚利桑那州凤凰城，服务于全球70多个国家和地区的客户。

8. **Cisco Systems** 思科系统

   全球最大的网络技术公司，于1984年12月在美国成立，总部设于加利福尼亚州硅谷的圣何塞，其产品涉及网络设备、软件、物联网、移动和无线网络、网络安全、音视频通信、数据中心、云计算等。

9. **Hewlett Packard Enterprise (HPE)** 慧与公司

   从惠普公司分拆并独立运营的一家财富500强上市公司，其业务范围主要涵盖服务器、存储、网络、软件、金融服务、咨询等，提供前沿的技术解决方案，帮助客户优化传统IT，打造安全的基于云且具备移动性的未来架构。

10. **Moore's Law** 摩尔定律

    摩尔定律指的是当价格不变时，集成电路上可容纳的元器件的数量，每隔18~24个月便会增加一倍，性能也将提升一倍。这一定律揭示了信息技术进步的速度。

→ Reading Skills

Surveying, Skimming and Scanning

Surveying a text is to take a broad look at the text, focusing on the general aspects, such as information about the author, date of publication, title, subtitle, introduction, and conclusion, rather than details. The main purpose is to determine the value of the text and whether or not it is worth reading more closely. For example, from the title of the text, "Despite Chip Shortage, Chip Innovation Is Booming", you can see that the text focuses on the field of chips, and then you can decide whether to proceed with your reading.

Skimming means reading quickly to get the gist of a text. It is concerned with finding general information, namely the main ideas. Therefore, it involves checking some elements like the first paragraph, the last paragraph, repeated words, section headings, the first sentence of each paragraph, and the last sentence of each paragraph. It helps you know what the text is all about at a basic level. Take the first paragraph as an example. It shows that a global shortage of semiconductors has a negative effect on carmakers and other companies but has a positive effect on Silicon Valley executives like Aart de Geus. The contrast sparks your interest in the reasons for the two opposite results. Then you go further to the first sentence of the second paragraph. It introduces the title of Aart de Geus, who comes from a representative company supplying software that engineers use to design chips. This information helps you get a brief idea of what the text is about, as well as a better understanding of the underlying importance of chips in this text.

Another important strategy for speed reading is scanning. Unlike skimming, scanning a text means going through it quickly to find specific information without reading all the details. To successfully scan a text, you need to first figure out how the text is organized. This is because it often gives you clues to identify which sections might contain the information you are looking for, such as time markers in a text arranged chronologically or subheadings in a text structured by themes. For this text, the most obvious feature is that it contains many proper nouns like company names, personal names and titles, which are helpful in locating relevant sections that need to be scanned. Second, it is important to keep the concept of key words in mind while scanning. Suppose you are looking for the answer to the question "What's the big change that has happened to the customers of Synopsys?" With proper scanning, you do not have to read every word or look at all the information. Just look for the terms "change" and "customers of Synopsys", and you can quickly find the answer in Para. 3.

→ Exercises

I. Building Vocabulary

Choose the best word in the box to fill in each blank. Use each word only once and make proper changes where necessary.

slump	venture	scramble	trickle	spike
span	veteran	massive	notorious	overriding

1. But the _____ priority for NATO seemed to be providing air support for outnumbered ground troops under continuous attack.

2. A(n) _____ in diabetes during pregnancy, worsened by the pandemic, raises the risk of chronic diabetes, heart disease, and birth complications.

3. According to Scanlon, the surprising success of Velocity at Discovery inspired the new _____ and the decision to launch as a free streaming network.

4. Hurricane Ian's _____ storm surge shows how the climate is changing due to sea level rise.

5. The store will _____ seven floors in a mixed-use, retail, hotel and high-rise residential tower.

6. If your project is opposed by, for example, a group of _____ employees, ask another old-timer to speak up for it.

7. Because of bottlenecks in the global supply chain, many stores are _____ to try to get all the inventory ahead of the crucial holiday shopping season.

8. The camp became _____ for the torture and inhumane treatment of its prisoners.

9. Meanwhile, the housing market continues to _____, with home builders sharply cutting back on construction projects.

10. Just 15 years ago, Singapore allowed only a(n) _____ of foreign newspapers into the country.

II. Understanding the Text

Skim and scan the text. Answer the following questions.

1. What does the author mean when he states that "Synopsys was showing its age until recently" in Para. 2?
2. What's the big change that has happened to the customers of Synopsys?
3. Why are venture capitalists traditionally not willing to invest in chip makers?
4. What is the writing purpose of Para. 8 and Para. 9?
5. In Para. 10, why did Jim Keller regard it as a "bloody miracle"?
6. How does the author illustrate that "the cycles should moderate"?
7. The text ends with the sentence "There you meet science fiction." What does it suggest?

III. Theme Exploration

Chips, semiconductors, and integrated circuits are important concepts in the field of electronics. As technology continues to develop, their application scopes and influences are also expanding. Discuss the relationship among them and their applications in our daily life.

IV. Real-Life Project

Semiconductor chips play an essential role in modern manufacturing, but the recent global shortage of chips has threatened the delivery of products ranging from PCs to automobiles to consumer electronics. What is causing this shortage? What effects does it bring about? When can we expect it to ease? Please search for relevant information and make a three-minute report on "Global Chip Shortage: Causes, Challenges, and Outlooks".

Introduction to Academic Writing

1. Definition of Academic Writing

Academic writing is a formal and rather impersonal style of writing used to communicate ideas and research in different disciplines. Intended for a specific audience, such as university students, academics, researchers, and practitioners within a field of study, academic writing is often found in journal papers and books on academic topics. Essays, research proposals, lab reports, theses, dissertations, and other documents for scholarly publication are also common genres that use it.

2. Basic Principles of Academic Writing

Although academic writing varies from discipline to discipline, and each academic genre has its unique conventions in terms of style, content, and format, there are basic principles that most academic writing follows:

• Being formal in style and cautious in tone. Academic writing should be formal and avoid casual or colloquial language.

• Being objective and unbiased. Academic writing is basically factual and unemotional. Its main purpose is to convey information clearly and impartially.

• Being well-sourced. Writers should support their claims with evidence from scholarly sources. Citations and referencing of related literature are essential in academic writing.

- Being focused and well-structured. Academic writing generally follows an organizational pattern with a clear focus and logical progression of ideas.

3. General Stylistic Features of English Academic Writing

Academic texts in different disciplines share some common stylistic features. Generally speaking, they are formal, objective, precise, and measured. These features are well reflected in the language used in academic writing.

1) Formal Language Instead of Informal Language

Informal language such as colloquialisms, contractions, and slang should be avoided in academic writing. Colloquialisms are words and phrases used in spoken English. *Don't*, *shouldn't*, *hasn't*, *isn't*, and *there's* are examples of contractions. To make writing more formal, academic writers use the full forms of these contractions. The table below lists some informal words and their formal equivalents. In academic writing, the formal words are preferred.

Informal	Formal	Informal	Formal	Informal	Formal
enough	sufficient	end	terminate	about	approximately
lack	deficiency	check	verify	tell	inform

2) Impersonal Language

The focus of academic writing is on the research problems being studied and the information being provided by the authors. Personal pronouns such as *I*, *we*, or *you* and expressions such as *in my opinion* are usually avoided to enhance the objective tone of academic writing. Compare the following sentences:

[1a] After discussing these cases, *we think* that falling is a serious matter among elderly people. (**personal**)

[1b] These cases show that falling is a serious matter among elderly people. (**impersonal**)

Emotive words or expressions should also be avoided in academic writing:

[2a] This *terrible tragedy* was *obviously* one of *the worst* catastrophes in construction history. (**emotive**)

[2b] The injury and mortality rates of this accident were among the highest in construction history. (**impersonal**)

3) Passive Voice

There are two types of voice in English grammar: active voice and passive voice. Although some language guidelines caution against the overuse of the passive voice, it is still frequently used in academic genres such as lab reports and scientific papers to convey objectivity and avoid the use of personal pronouns. Look at the passive voice used in the following sentences:

[3] The study *was conducted* using a total of 20 mice randomly divided into 4 groups.

[4] As *can be seen* from the data, two-thirds of the respondents are satisfied with the current provision.

4) Single Verbs Instead of Phrasal Verbs

Both phrasal verbs and single verbs can be used to express an action or occurrence in English (Swales & Feak, 2012). Phrasal verbs usually consist of two words, such as *make up* and *take on*, and single verbs are either English or Latin-based verbs. Because phrasal verbs tend to have various meanings depending on the context, they are considered less precise and are often used in spoken language or less formal written texts. In academic writing, it is preferable to use single verbs rather than phrasal verbs for formality and precision. Here are some examples:

[5] Western scholars gradually *turned out* a corpus of translations from Arabic and studies of Islam. (*produced*)

[6] Modern research is also *looking into* vaccine therapy against cancer. (*investigating*)

5) Nominalization

Nominalization occurs quite frequently in academic writing. It is the formation of nouns from verbs or adjectives and noun phrases from clauses. Nominalization allows writers to pack more information into sentences, making writing more concise. In addition, appropriate use of nominalization helps to maintain an objective and impersonal tone in academic writing. Compare the sentences on the next page to understand how nominalization contributes to formal writing.

Sentences without nominalization	Sentences with nominalization
The report shows that we could boost conservation efforts by combining space-based imaging and artificial intelligence.	The report shows that the combination of space-based imaging and artificial intelligence could boost conservation efforts.
The number of people consuming fast food increased significantly in 2015.	There was a significant increase in the number of people consuming fast food in 2015.

6) Hedges

According to *The Academic Phrasebank* at the University of Manchester, one of the most noticeable stylistic features of academic writing is the tendency of writers to avoid absolute certainty and over-generalization. Writers are encouraged to be thoughtful and cautious when interpreting research findings, giving implications or recommendations, and making claims. Linguistic devices used to reduce the strength of a statement or claim are known as hedging devices. The following table shows different types of hedges.

Types	Examples of hedges	Sentences
modal lexical verbs	seem, tend, appear, assume, suggest, estimate	The results *seemed to* depend on the period of exposure.
modal auxiliaries	can, could, may, might, would, should	The heat waves *could* be attributed to the El Nino weather phenomenon.
modal nouns	suggestion, assumption, claim, possibility, probability	One *assumption* is that the biological activity of any DNA administered is directly proportional to the amount of that DNA.
adverbs of probability	perhaps, possibly, probably, presumably	The second reason is *probably* more fundamental.
adjectives of probability	probable, possible, likely, unlikely	It is *probable* that this initial misstep will be repeated.
approximators of degree, quantity, and frequency	roughly, to some extent, approximately, occasionally, generally	These findings *generally* support Davis' cognitive behavioral model of Internet addiction.
"It" phrases	It might suggest that..., It can be argued that..., It seems reasonable to assume that...	*It seems reasonable to assume that* pragmatic factors in comprehension will also be present in production.

Unit 1 Smart World, Better World

(Continued)

Types	Examples of hedges	Sentences
expressions indicating the writer's distance	based on, according to, in the view of, on the evidence of	The evaluation of mineral or petroleum potential is an interpretation *based on* the data available.

→ Exercises

I. **Replace each underlined phrasal verb with a single verb to reduce the informality of the sentence. Change the form of the single verb where necessary.**

1. Thompson <u>points out</u> that the increase in life expectancy has led to some economic problems.

   _____

2. Enrollment <u>went up</u> rapidly during the 2022–2023 academic year.

   _____

3. In addition, the questions focused on the measures taken by the New Zealand government to <u>get rid of</u> child poverty.

   _____

II. **Rewrite the following sentences using nominalization.**

1. Many animal species have become extinct because their natural habitats have been destroyed.

   _____

2. We analyzed the data from the experiment and it revealed that children react when they have too much sugar.

   _____

3. They studied how malaria disseminates due to poor housing and infrastructure.

   _____

III. Read the following paragraphs. Underline any non-academic expressions and rewrite them in a more academic style.

1. Some people think contemporary art is getting worse. They say this has been going on for quite a long time. I think they are right, because now we have bad artworks and funny displays in museums and galleries all the time.

_____

_____

2. There're 50 online ads with about 601 tokens in our data. And these ads were mainly chosen from three SM platforms: Instagram, Snapchat, and Twitter. They were published in recent three years. Why do we choose our data from these three famous platforms? This is because they are very popular and there're more than 1 billion active users on them. So this can ensure that our data is authentic and valid.

_____

_____

Part III
Translating

学术英语翻译概述

一、汉英语言对比

　　语言是文化的重要组成部分，本质上是文化的反映。语言差异源于文化差异，不同语言的交流实质上是不同文化的交流。中国的农本文化提倡人与自然和谐相处，天人合一，主张集体利益高于个人利益，重人本，思维上具有具象和综合性的特点。而英美为代表的西方商业文化则提倡同类竞争以求生存，独立开放以及看重个体价值，重器物，思维上具有理性和分析性的特点。这种文化差异可反映在语言使用的多个方面，下面以词汇和句法结构为例进行说明。

Unit 1 Smart World, Better World

1. 词汇方面

（1）汉语词义一般较笼统，而英语词义往往较具体。例如"酒"一词，汉语中可以指所有经过发酵制成的含酒精的饮品，而英语习惯用具体的 beer（啤酒）、wine（葡萄酒）、cocktail（鸡尾酒）、champagne（香槟）、margarita（玛格丽塔）、whisky（威士忌）、rum（朗姆）、brandy（白兰地）等词表示不同种类的酒。

（2）汉语词汇形象性强，很有画面感。例如，"蚕食"（nibble）、"怒发冲冠"（bristle with anger），而对应的英语词汇多注重表达所指的功能与逻辑，形象性缺失。

（3）汉语是动态性语言，而英语中很多意义常通过静态方式表达，体现在多用名词、介词、形容词及其短语。比较以下中英文例句：

| Solar panels are already a familiar sight on rooftops. | 太阳能电池板在屋顶上已随处可见。 |
| They seem to have lost sight of the fact that marketing is only a means to an end. | 他们似乎忽略了这样一个事实：营销只是达到目的的手段。 |

英语的静态性还体现在名词化结构的使用上，常用抽象名词来表达动作、行为、状态、特征等，这也是学术英语的一个重要文体特征。

| The compression of the soil under the applied stresses would force some water out of the voids. | 施加压力压缩土壤会使一些水从孔隙中排出。 |
| Participation in Organic and Fair Trade networks reduces farmers' livelihood vulnerability. | 加入有机食品和公平交易网络后，农民的生活便不再那么艰难。 |

2. 句法方面

（1）从句子结构上看，英语句子常用无生命的词作主语，倾向于客观表达事物作用的结果。汉语多用有生命的词语作主语，从人的角度来叙述主体思维，倾向于描述人的行为或感受。

| The prevalence of the disease is a source of confusion among health experts. | 卫生专家对该疾病的流行感到困惑。 |
| His failure to respond to the criticism only made matters worse. | 他未能对批评做出回应，结果只是让事情变得更糟。 |

（2）英语句子使用被动语态的频率要大大高于汉语句子。

| It is estimated that more than 99% of the matter in the universe exists in the plasma state. | 据估计，宇宙中 99% 以上的物质以等离子体的状态存在。 |
| The sodium hydroxide was dissolved in water. This solution was then titrated with hydrochloric acid. | 将氢氧化钠溶解在水中，然后用盐酸滴定溶液。 |

（3）英语句子中的修饰语如果是短语或分句，往往放在被修饰语之后，形成英语句子"重后饰"的特点。汉语的修饰语常常处于被修饰成分之前。

These are the projects that scientists are thinking about and even working on, but are hampered by lack of resources.	这些是科学家们正在思考甚至正在从事的项目，但却因为缺乏资源而受阻。
The first wave of modern AI systems, which emerged a decade ago, relied on carefully labelled training data.	十年前出现的第一波现代人工智能系统依赖于精心标记的训练数据。

（4）英语中带有长修饰语的句子较为常见，句子可能既长又复杂，就像竹子一样，许多枝叶都长在一个主干上。相比之下，汉语句子的结构相对简单，汉语的长句常常被分割成短句甚至短语。

Data-center chips are bright spot in an otherwise dark year for the semiconductor industry, which is in the grip of a cyclical downturn that has wiped two-fifths from the market value of the world's chipmakers this year.	数据中心芯片是身处黑暗之年的半导体行业的一个亮点。半导体行业正处于周期性低迷期，这使得今年全球芯片制造商的市值蒸发了五分之二。

（5）英语是一种形合（hypotaxis）语言，常借助词汇手段（衔接词）和形态手段（派生、屈折等变化）实现句子内部和句子之间的衔接。汉语则是一种意合（parataxis）语言，即可以不借助语言形式手段而依靠词语或句子间的语义联系来实现词语或句子的衔接。

In agriculture, for example, as the Mineral Rover moves through a field, it uses artificial intelligence to measure leaf size and fruit count which can help farmers increase crops.	例如，在农业领域，当矿物探测车在田间穿行时，通过人工智能来测量叶子的大小和果实的数量，可以帮助农民增加作物产量。

二、学术英语翻译基本原则

学术英语主要应用于研究、学习、教学等领域，其用语规范，语气正式，具有客观性、逻辑性和专业性强等特点。因此，翻译学术英语时首先必须准确规范，忠实地传达原文的全部信息。其次，译文还要符合学术英语特定的文体风格和语言特征。翻译学术英语时，我们应遵循以下几条原则：

1. 斟酌词义，力求准确

翻译时要特别注意学术词汇在不同学科领域中的准确含义。例如：

[1] Your primitives are literally moving pieces of data from one location of memory to another, through a very simple **operation**（操作）. (computer science)

Unit 1 Smart World, Better World

[2] Doctors in training may have to do hundreds of stitches in some cases to close the skin after an **operation**（手术）. (medicine)

[3] That is the **operation**（运作过程）of the gas discharge tube. (chemistry)

学术英语中不同的词语搭配会产生不同的意义，翻译时要注意这种搭配意义，采用准确且符合学科规范的表述。例如：

idle asset	闲置资产	*develop* AIDS	患艾滋病
idle state	空闲状态	*develop* film	冲洗胶片
idle speed	空转速度；怠速	*develop* vaccine	研制疫苗
idle wheel/gear	惰轮	*develop* agriculture	发展农业

2. 逻辑严密，力求简洁

学术文本条理性、逻辑性强，翻译时要保证译文准确通顺，译者需厘清错综复杂的成分和句子之间的逻辑关系，且译文要符合译入语的表达习惯。由于英汉语言系统的差异，译入语与源语可以不用一一对应，但译者要尽可能使用精炼的词句清楚地传达原文意图。以下三种译文中，译文 A 既体现了主从句之间的逻辑关系，语言表述上也更清楚简洁。

> As friction manifests itself as a resistance that opposes motion, it is usually considered as a nuisance.
> A. 摩擦表现为运动的阻力，因此常被人看成讨厌的东西。
> B. 由于摩擦表现为抵抗运动的阻力，因此通常被视为一种讨厌的现象。
> C. 由于摩擦本身显示了阻碍运动的阻力，因此，通常被看成是运动过程中的障碍。

→ Exercises

I. Translate the following sentences into Chinese.

1. He is more comfortable with computers than with people.

2. a. Eventually the new systems were designed to operate on alternating current.

   b. By slowing or stopping this ocean current, global warming would actually cool

Europe dramatically.

c. Wind is an air current caused by a vacuum created by hot air rising.

II. **Compare and translate the following passages. Appreciate their stylistic differences.**

1. a. What a piece of work is a man! How noble in reason! How infinite in faculties! In form and moving, how express and admirable! In action, how like an angel!

   b. Man is metazoan, triploblastic, vertebrate, pentadactyl, mammalian, eutherian, primate... The main outline of each of his principal system of organs may be traced back, like those of other mammals, to the fishes.

2. a. Important studies have shown that time spent outdoors can delay the onset or even reduce the progression of myopia. More research needs to be performed but the amount of time spent outside appears to at least be an important risk factor. The reason why this is true may be related to a reduction in obesity, an increase in vitamin D production, socialized games that occur outside or may even be related to dopamine levels in the body. One of the strongest mechanisms of action currently being studied is the amount of sun exposure or the amount of illumination or simply brightness that you receive while outside.

   b. Children are spending less time outdoors than previous generations. Being outdoors, in the presence of sunlight, has a protective effect against nearsightedness. This could be due to the brightness of the light, looking long distance, or could be due to the exposure of UV or violet-white light on the eye

Unit 1 Smart World, Better World

and retina. A child should ideally spend at least two hours a day outdoors to reduce the risk of becoming nearsighted.

Unit 2

Living with AI

Part I
Reading

The Move from Old-School Manufacturing to Smart Manufacturing

John Clemons

① The goal of smart manufacturing is to help the manufacturing industry become a driving force in the economy once again. That said, smart manufacturing is completely different from old-school manufacturing and has completely changed the manufacturing landscape.

② In order to understand how smart manufacturing can enhance your existing operations and help you move into the modern world, this article looks at the differences between smart manufacturing and old-school manufacturing, as well as how manufacturing leaders can make the *transition*.

Capacity vs. Capability

③ Old-school manufacturing is about how much *capacity* a plant has and how to get more capacity. There are lots of *metrics* around capacity, like overall equipment effectiveness (OEE), which is often used to find ways to increase capacity without adding additional equipment or lines.

④ With smart manufacturing, it's about what the plant can do. How can we grow our capabilities? Capabilities like the ability to make different products, change products quickly, respond quickly to requests from customers, easily adopt new processes and easily and quickly make new products.

⑤ To get started with this transition, start small and *customize* your products, adding data and services to them. This should enable you to solve problems and provide solutions for your customers instead of providing them only with products and services.

Low-Cost Labor vs. Knowledge Worker

⑥   The old-school manufacturing **mindset** focuses on low-cost labor as a **commodity** that you can buy in bulk whenever you need it—and get a **bulk discount**. The cheaper, the better, no matter the skill level.

⑦   Smart manufacturing, on the other hand, is about data, information, and knowledge. A modern facility requires smart technology and smart people to run it. People who are hired for their ability to think, analyze, **synthesize**, create, learn, and adapt in a modern world.

⑧   The challenge is finding and **retaining** the right people. As more employees are retiring and fewer people are pursuing careers in manufacturing, manufacturers must be **proactive** in capturing knowledge from retiring employees. They must train employees on new technologies and tools and ensure workers have the information they need when they need it.

⑨   A good first step in attracting and retaining highly skilled people is to make the **commitment** to a modern digital work environment and demonstrate you are capable of adopting smart tools and technologies.

Mass Production vs. The Digital Factory

⑩   Henry Ford made mass production into an art form and added the famous **tagline** that customers could have a car in any color they wanted if it was black. It's about making large numbers of **duplicate** products. Mass production was good because it allowed Ford to get the cost of automobiles down to where everyone could afford one.

⑪   In today's competitive climate, the business model has changed from mass production to **customization**. People want exactly what they want, and it's often different from what everyone else wants. That's what the digital factory is about—making unique and individual items even to the point of making just one and customizing it to exact **specifications**.

⑫   The digital factory provides a path forward from mass production to a more modern process. With smart technologies and devices, knowledge workers have access to real-time data about what happened and why. They can then use this data to make more informed decisions about facility operations and processes.

⑬   For a more data-driven approach, look at technologies, such as AI, machine learning, data *analytics*, digital twins/threads, the IIoT and more to provide you with the ability to access data and turn it into intelligence to be used and shared.

Productivity vs. Agility and Responsiveness

⑭   Old-school manufacturing is also about productivity and how to increase it. Lots and lots of metrics revolve around productivity. Most continuous improvement programs are about improving productivity. In the end, the focus tends to be more on the number of products produced versus the labor hours required to produce the products. Obviously, the more products produced with fewer labor hours, the better.

⑮   As the focus shifts from increased productivity to making the right product to customer specifications, being *agile* and responsive is a key factor for operations. *Agility* is being able to move quickly to new products, new materials, and new processes to support responsiveness, which is about making sure you respond to the customer and provide them with exactly what they want and when they want it.

⑯   That's what satisfies customers, and that process is what will help your company *thrive* in today's world.

Capacity Fulfillment vs. Customer Fulfillment

⑰   Finally, old-school manufacturing is about capacity *fulfillment*. You see this in the sales and marketing side of the business when everyone is just trying to sell out the capacity of the plant using discounts, promotions, and other sales and marketing *gimmicks*.

⑱   Today, the focus is on customer fulfillment—meeting their needs, as opposed to simply selling them something. *Leveraging* smart technologies, you can use intelligent, real-time data to understand the customer and then change the plant, products, materials or process to meet their needs. You should be able to provide real value to the customer above and beyond what they get from other suppliers—and deliver that value to them how, when, and where they want it.

⑲   It's not easy, and it requires a huge change in the way you think about your manufacturing plants and in the way you run your manufacturing plants. In the end, the value that you provide the customer and the long-term relationship you create with the customer far *outweighs* any short-term challenges you have in manufacturing.

Conclusion

20　Smart manufacturing really is helping manufacturing once again become a driving force in the economy. It's doing it through new ideas and new technologies. It's doing it through smart people and smart technologies. It's not old-school manufacturing; in fact, it's a completely different *outlook* about what manufacturing is supposed to be.

→ Words and Expressions

transition *n.* the process or a period of changing from one state or condition to another 转变，转换

capacity *n.* the amount of something that a factory, company, machine, etc. can produce or deal with 生产能力；容量

metrics *n.* a standard of measurement 度量；指标

customize *vt.* to change something to make it more suitable for you, or to make it look special or different from things of a similar type 定制，改制（以满足顾主的需要）

mindset *n.* someone's general attitude, and the way in which they think about things and make decisions 观念模式，思维倾向

commodity *n.* a product that is bought and sold 商品，货物

bulk discount a lower price that is offered for buying a large number or amount of something 大宗购买折扣；批发价

synthesize *vt.* to combine separate things into a complete whole 综合；结合

retain *vt.* if a company retains workers, it continues to employ them for a long time 留用（员工）

proactive *adj.* doing something to influence or make changes happen and being prepared for change to happen 积极主动的

commitment *n.* a promise to do something or to behave in a particular way 保证，承诺

tagline *n.* the last few words in a television or radio advertisement 品牌口号；宣传语

duplicate *adj.* [only before noun] exactly the same as something, or made as an exact copy of something 完全一样的

customization *n.* the action of making or changing something according to the buyer's or user's needs 定制；定制化服务

specification *n.* [usually plural] a detailed instruction about how a car, building, piece of equipment, etc. should be made 规格；具体要求

analytics *n.* the discovery and communication of meaningful patterns in data 分析法

agile *adj.* (business) used to describe a way of working in which the time and place of work, and the roles that people carry out, can all be changed according to need, and the focus is on the goals to be achieved, rather than the exact methods used 灵活的；（工作中）见机行事的，反应快速的

agility *n.* ways of planning and doing work in which it is understood that making changes as they are needed is an important part of the job （工作中）见机行事，反应快速

thrive *vi.* to become very successful or very strong and healthy 兴旺；茁壮成长

fulfillment *n.* the act of doing or achieving what was hoped for or expected 实现；满足

gimmick *n.* something that is not serious or of real value that is used to attract people's attention or interest temporarily, especially to make them buy something （尤指为诱人购买而搞的）花招，把戏

leverage *vt.* to spread or use resources (money, skills, buildings, etc. that an organization has available), ideas, etc. again in several different ways or in different parts of a company, system, etc. 最大限度利用，最优化使用

outweigh *vt.* to be more important or valuable than something else （在重要性或意义上）超过

outlook *n.* your general attitude to life and the world 观点，看法，见解

→ Notes

1. **John Clemons** 约翰·克莱蒙斯
   福布斯理事会成员，罗克韦尔自动化公司和 Maverick Technologies 顾问。Maverick Technologies 是工业自动化、企业集成、运营咨询和维护服务提供商。该公司在全球拥有 500 多名员工和 18 个美国办事处，是北美最大的独立系统集成商。

2. **OEE**（Overall Equipment Effectiveness）整体设备效率
   评估生产设施有效运作的指数。其计算结果是通用的，甚至可以用来比较不同行业。整体设备效率也可以作为关键绩效指标和精益生产的效率指标。

3. **Henry Ford** 亨利·福特
   美国汽车工程师与企业家，福特汽车公司的建立者。亨利·福特是世界上第一位将装配线概念实际应用在工厂并大量生产而获得巨大成功者，他让汽车在美国真正普及化。

4. **digital twins** 数字孪生
   数字孪生是充分利用物理模型、传感器更新、运行历史等数据，集成多学科、多物理量、多尺度、多概率的仿真过程，在虚拟空间中完成映射，从而反映相对应的实体装备的全生命周期过程。

5. **digital threads** 数字线程
   数字线程是数字孪生技术体系中的核心技术，它是一种通信框架，用来展示资产数据在整个生命周期（从原材料到最终产品）的互联的数据流和集成视图。

6. **IIoT**（Industrial Internet of Things）工业物联网
   工业物联网是面向制造业数字化、网络化、智能化需求，将互联感测器、仪表以及其他设备和工业应用程序通过网络连接形成的系统。该网络用于实现海量数据采集、交换和智能分析，从而大幅提升生产效率和经济效益。

→ Reading Skills

Recognizing Text Patterns of Organization

When writing texts, authors often organize supporting details in a particular pattern to ensure effective communication of ideas for potential readers. A clear pattern of organization provides focus and direction, avoids chaos and confusion, and facilitates the smooth decoding of information. Therefore, it is crucial for a reader to recognize the organization patterns when reading texts.

There are many patterns writers can use to organize their ideas, but there is no fixed rule for choosing a suitable organizational pattern. Which specific pattern to choose depends on the topic and the writing purpose of the text. The most commonly used patterns of organization are *Definition and Example, Time/*

Chronological Order, Classification, Comparison and Contrast, Problem and Solution, Cause and Effect, Listing and *Process*.

This text is organized in the pattern of comparison and contrast. Generally speaking, the compare-contrast organizational pattern is used in the cases where one subject is described and compared with another. From the title of the text, "The Move from Old-School Manufacturing to Smart Manufacturing," we can easily tell that the purpose of the text is to make a comparison between two modes of manufacturing.

There are two ways to organize a comparison and contrast essay. The first (and often the clearest) method is the Point-by-Point method, and the second method is called the Block method. The Point-by-Point method alternates arguments about the two items (A and B) compared and/or contrasted, while the Block method presents all arguments related to A, and then compares and/or contrasts them to all arguments related to B. This text is clearly organized in the Point-by-Point method with the help of the subtitles, such as *Capacity Vs. Capability* and *Low-Cost Labor Vs. Knowledge Worker*. This method is often easier for a reader to follow because similarities and differences are more obvious when placed next to each other. For this reason, writers generally use this method for longer essays.

→ Exercises

I. Building Vocabulary

Choose the best word in the box to fill in each blank. Use each word only once and make proper changes where necessary.

agile	thrive	mindset	retain	fulfillment
outlook	proactive	commitment	outweigh	duplicate

1. Steve Jobs was not a technical wizard, but he thoroughly understood the _____ of the people who were.

2. Even if a few people would take the cash without contributing to society, the

benefits may substantially _____ the costs.

3. Honda does have plans to electrify the Super Cub, but is seeing its market shrinking thanks to more _____ Chinese competitors moving much faster.

4. Companies that can _____ their employees will find that onboarding and upskilling become quicker.

5. Labor needs to match its _____ to spending with innovative ideas about service delivery, financing and management.

6. To help the supply and customer chains _____, the owners work with importers to source unique coffee bean businesses in nearly every coffee-growing country.

7. Every day, women strive harder than ever before in order to discover _____ in every area of their life.

8. Building trust with your clients requires you to be _____ about addressing their needs—not just reacting to requests.

9. Nearly everyone had a very positive _____ and the plans for action to revive the area were discussed.

10. Keep a set of _____ keys in a safe place, in case you lose the originals.

II. Understanding the Text

This text describes smart manufacturing and old-school manufacturing in the pattern of comparison and contrast. Find out their similarities and differences, and then fill in the diagram. Do more research for further information if necessary.

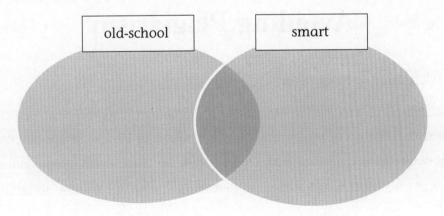

III. Theme Exploration

As the writer states, smart manufacturing has completely changed the manufacturing landscape, and it is creating a more agile and productive industrial base. However, the widespread industry adoption of smart manufacturing still faces barriers, especially for small-to-medium manufacturing enterprises (SMEs), due to cost and lack of workforce training.

Work in groups and search for relevant information, and then discuss how to deal with the problem from your point of view.

IV. Real-Life Project

Rob Gorham, the executive director of the Secure America Institute, said that "Smart manufacturing is a national priority as detailed in the White House Critical and Emerging Technologies Report". Obviously, the United States has attached great importance to smart manufacturing. What about the situation in China? In terms of smart manufacturing, what has been achieved? What problems are to be solved? What is the greatest difficulty or challenge? Do some research on the current situation of smart manufacturing in China, and then make a three-minute report on "Smart Manufacturing in China".

Part II
Writing

Avoiding Plagiarism

1. Definition of Plagiarism

According to *Publication Manual of the American Psychological Association*, "plagiarism is the act of presenting the words, ideas, or images of another as one's own; it denies authors credit where credit is due." In other words, plagiarism occurs when a person takes words, ideas, or images from a source without appropriately acknowledging the original author. Whether deliberate or accidental, plagiarism is a violation of academic integrity and is viewed as academic theft.

2. Common Types of Plagiarism

In academic writing, plagiarism may occur in different forms. Some of the most common types include:

- **Direct plagiarism:** a word-for-word copy of words or sentences from someone else's work without acknowledging the source or using quotation marks.

- **Patchwork plagiarism:** copying phrases, passages, or ideas from various existing sources and rearranging them to create a new text without citing the sources.

- **Self-plagiarism:** taking one's own previously written work, either in full or in part, and presenting it as new without citing the source.

- **Accidental plagiarism:** plagiarism that occurs through avoidable mistakes such as forgetting quotation marks, misquoting original sources, or inadequately paraphrasing another person's idea(s).

3. Ways to Avoid Plagiarism

One essential feature of academic writing is its dependence on the work of other researchers and writers. Academic norms require writers to cite sources when referring to relevant literature and when borrowing ideas or words from others. Citing sources honestly and appropriately is not only a safe practice for writers to avoid plagiarism, but also helps to enhance the integrity and credibility of their academic work. There are three ways of incorporating borrowed words and ideas into another work: quoting, paraphrasing, and summarizing. They involve different levels of borrowing.

1) Quoting

Quoting means taking the exact words from an original source with the use of quotation marks and the citation of source information. Direct quotations are effective in some situations, for example, when exact wording is needed for technical accuracy or when the source's authority gives weight to an argument. Here is an example:

Original text	Example of quoting
Material qualities can also acquire meaning, not on the basis of where they come from, but on the basis of our physical, bodily experience of them. (**Source:** Kress, G. & Van Leeuwen, T. (2001). *Multimodal Discourse: The Modes and Media of Contemporary Communication.* London: Edward Arnold.)	According to **Kress & Van Leeuwen (2001)**, "Material qualities can also acquire meaning, not on the basis of where they come from, but on the basis of our physical, bodily experience of them." (p. 74)

Quoting directly is straightforward, however, it should be done sparingly and used only when necessary. Paraphrasing and summarizing, also referred to as two indirect ways of citing sources, are more commonly used to avoid plagiarism.

2) Paraphrasing

Paraphrasing aims to restate the ideas taken from another source in one's own words without changing the original meaning. A paraphrase is usually close in length to the original text. Compared with quoting, paraphrasing can help writers understand the source material on a deeper level. There is no need to use quotation marks when paraphrasing, but it is still necessary to credit the source properly. Besides, to preserve the original meaning, no personal comments or evaluations should be added. Here are some strategies for paraphrasing:

• Read the source text carefully and list the ideas in the text.

• Identify the meaning relationships between the ideas (e.g., cause/effect, generalization, contrast) and express the relationships in a new way.

• Restate the ideas by changing both the words (except for technical terms) and sentence structures: Substitute the original words with synonyms or alternative expressions; change parts of speech or voices; change sentences to phrases and vice versa.

• Acknowledge the source.

Look at how the strategies are used in the following example:

Original text	Example of paraphrasing
Engaging with animals was perceived to be more useful than exposure to the stress prevention content presentations because the presence of animals created a more positive and calming environment. (**Source:** Pendry, P., Carr, A. M., Gee, N. R., & Vandagriff, J. L. (2020). Randomized trial examining effects of animal assisted intervention and stress related symptoms on college students' learning and study skills. *International Journal of Environmental Research and Public Health, 17*(6), 1909.)	**Pendry et al. (2020) hold that** as animals can make a space feel welcoming and soothing, students can experience more mental health benefits by interacting with therapy animals than attending presentations about stress prevention.

3) Summarizing

Summarizing is creating a condensed version of a source text by identifying the main points and presenting them in one's own words. A summary is significantly shorter than the original work. Its length may range from just a sentence to hundreds of words, depending on the specific writing purpose. Summarizing is useful in academic writing, especially when an author wants to cite others' ideas using fewer words or provide a brief overview of other researchers' work. Like a paraphrase, a summary must be neutral without any involvement of the summary writer's personal bias or comments. The following strategies can help create a good summary:

• Read the source text carefully and understand it thoroughly.

• Highlight the relevant essential information according to the summary writer's purpose.

• Underline key words, including key transitional elements.

• Make a note of the main points, eliminating unnecessary details, examples, and explanations.

• Restate the main points by changing both the words (except for technical terms) and sentence structures: Substitute the original words with synonyms or alternative expressions; change parts of speech or voices; reduce complex sentences to simple sentences, simple sentences to phrases, and phrases to single words.

• Reorganize the main points into a coherent passage.

• Acknowledge the source.

Look at how the strategies are used in the following example:

Original text	Example of summarizing
There is widespread fear that AI-powered machines will automate many familiar office tasks and displace many jobs. This fear is not unique to AI technology. For hundreds of years, new technologies have stirred social unrest when workers felt threatened by loss of their jobs and livelihoods. The fear is heightened in the modern age by the accelerated pace of AI automation. A century ago, a technology change was a slow process that took a generation to be fully adopted. Today, a technology change can appear as an avalanche, sweeping away jobs, identities, and professions in just a few years. (**Source:** Denning, P. J. & Denning, D. E. (2020). Dilemmas of artificial intelligence. *Communications of the ACM, 63*(3), 22–24.)	Technology development has been a threat of unemployment for centuries. In the past, people reconciled themselves to its slow change, while in modern times, people have an intensified anxiety about job displacement due to the explosive growth of technology, especially progress in AI (**Denning & Denning, 2020**).

→ Exercises

I. Study the following academic situations and decide which is plagiarism.

1. Using statistics from someone else's work without crediting the source.

   _____

2. Using widely known scientific or historical facts without citation.

   _____

3. Rewording a paragraph but keeping its sentence structure without crediting the original author.

   _____

4. Borrowing skeletal phrases that are frequently used in academic English.

   _____

5. Using someone's quotes or copying the exact paragraph without giving quotation marks.

   _____

II. **Read the two paraphrases of the original text below. Choose the one that better paraphrases the original text and state your reasons.**

【Original text】"In psychology, an understanding of the methods psychologists use is important because research can be flawed, and knowing how research should be done can bring those flaws to light" (Ciccarelli & White, 2009, p. 3).

【Version 1】In the field of psychology, understanding the research methods psychologists use is essential because research can be defective, and understanding how research should be done can bring those imperfections to light.

【Version 2】To understand potential weaknesses in research, it's important to understand the methods used by psychologists (Ciccarelli & White, 2009).

III. **Paraphrase the following passage.**

Organizations are trying to become more competitive and efficient by transforming themselves into digital firms where nearly all core business process and relationships with customers, suppliers, and employees are digitally managed. (Source: Laudon, K. C. & Laudon, J. P. (2004). *Management Information Systems: Managing the Digital Firm* (9th Edition). Upper Saddle River: Prentice Hall.)

_____

_____

IV. **Write a one-sentence summary for the following text.**

The booming science of decision making has shown that more information can lead to objectively poorer choices, and to choices that people come to regret. It has shown that an unconscious system guides many of our decisions, and that it can be sidelined by too much information. And it has shown that decisions requiring creativity benefit from letting the problem incubate below the level of awareness—something that becomes ever more difficult when information never stops arriving. (Source: Sharon Begley. (2011, Feb. 27). The science of making decisions. *Newsweek*.)

_____

_____

_____

Part III
Translating

术语翻译和词性转换

一、术语翻译

Peter Newmark（2001）认为，技术翻译与其他类型翻译的主要区别在于术语。使用专业术语是学术英语文章的一个重要特征，这些术语数量庞大，翻译时需要把握词义的准确性。专业术语一般有以下两种来源：

1. 纯专业术语

这类术语词义单一，适用范围狭窄，多用于特定专业领域。有些是从拉丁语或希腊语演变而来，例如：algorithm（算法）、geometry（几何）、anemia（贫血）、mitochondria（线粒体）。还有一些专业术语是随着科技或学科发展而出现的新词，这些词可以通过派生（affixation）、合成（compounding）、缩略（acronym）、混合（blending）等构词法获得。例如：macrometeorology（宏观气象学）、virtual reality（虚拟现实）、COVID-19（新型冠状病毒肺炎）、cablegram（海底电报）。

2. 半专业术语

这类词主要来源于日常用语，用在不同的专业领域具有不同的词义，例如：power（功率；幂方）、condenser（发电厂；冷凝器；聚光器）、core（地核；关键职能）。

针对其特点和来源，在翻译专业术语时可采用以下几种方法：

（1）音译法：即把原术语用译入语中相同或相近发音的词翻译出来。某些新技术、新概念或新材料在出现之初较多使用音译法，某些学科中的计量单位词一般也用音译法。例如：karst（喀斯特）、watt（瓦特）、El Nino（厄尔尼诺）、ounce（盎司）、calorie（卡路里）、sonar（声呐）。

（2）意译法：与音译法相比，意译法更能清晰准确地表达术语的内涵。它通过对原术语所表达的概念进行准确分析后，译出各部分的意思。例如：blockchain（区块链）、AR（增强现实）、thermal couple（热电偶）。

（3）意音结合法：在音译之后加上一个表示类别的词，或者把原词的一部分音译，而另一部分意译。例如：Doppler effect（多普勒效应）、megavolt（百万伏）、dural（杜拉铝）、radar-man（雷达兵）、cartoon（卡通片）。

（4）形译法：某些术语由大写字母加名词构成，大写字母表示事物的形状，名词表示事物的性质。汉译时可以把字母翻译成形状相近的文字，也可以保留大写字母，只翻译名词，还可以把大写字母翻译成可以体现其形状的文字。例如：Type I model（工字模型）、Z-iron（乙字铁）、inverted-T bent cap（倒T形桩帽）、U-bar（U形杆）、O-ring（密封圈）、L-square（直角板）。

（5）零翻译：在科技文献中，商标、牌号、型号和表示特定意义的字母均可不译，直接使用原文，只译普通名词。例如：ACI 318–14 effectiveness factor（ACI 318–14 准则有效系数）。

二、词性转换

词性转换是一种常用的翻译技巧，它能使译文富有表现力且更自然通顺。由于英汉两种语言在语法和用法上的差异，翻译实践过程中，很多时候都需要进行词性转换，即将原文中属于某一类词性的词转换为译文中另一类词性的词。理论上词性转换可以在任意两种词性中应用，然而在实践中主要是将不同词性的英语词转换成汉语动词、名词、形容词和副词。

1. 转换成汉语动词

（1）名词转换成动词

| The need for a second substitute would require the case to be reheard from the beginning. | 如有必要再次替换（法官），案件则须从头开始重新听讯。 |
| Many delegations urged a continued application and refinement of the results-based programming approach. | 许多代表团要求继续采用并改进基于结果的计划编制法。 |

（2）形容词转换为动词

| The Secretariat has already become less dependent on printed documents which results in a better and more efficient use of the available resources. | 秘书处已经不那么依赖打印文件了，这样可以更好更有效地利用可用资源。 |
| The international community must remain alert to the possible direct and indirect security implications of climate change. | 国际社会必须继续警惕气候变化可能带来的直接和间接安全影响。 |

（3）副词转换为动词

The experiment in chemistry was 10 minutes behind.	这个化学实验延误了十分钟。
Data were collected using two quantitative questionnaires administered at least two months apart.	采用两份定量问卷收集数据，两次调查至少间隔2个月。

（4）介词转换成动词

By increasing the pressure upon a gas, the volume of it can get smaller.	当增大施加在气体上的压力时，气体的体积就缩小。
The letter E is commonly used for electromotive force.	通常用字母E表示电势能。

2. 转换成汉语名词

（1）动词转换成名词

The black hole weighs about 400 times as much as the sun.	这个黑洞的重量约为太阳重量的400倍。
However, these institutes and centers may differ considerably, in terms of their administrative procedures and needs, from the field offices.	不过，这些研究所和中心在行政管理程序和需求方面与驻外办事处之间的差别可能会很大。

（2）形容词转换成名词

There are a range of environmental impacts associated with the operation of nuclear power installations, not all of which are radioactive in nature.	核电设施在运作过程中对环境产生一系列影响，但并非都具有放射性。
Oil is not as dense as water and it therefore floats.	油的密度比水小，因此可以浮起来。

3. 转换成汉语形容词

（1）副词转换成形容词

The activities of international intergovernmental and non-governmental organizations relating to space law had continued to contribute significantly to the study, clarification and development of space law.	国际政府间组织和非政府组织在空间法方面的活动继续对研究、阐释和制定空间法做出重要的贡献。
This innovative solution is chiefly characterized by modifications to the steering system.	这一创新解决方案的主要特征是对转向系统进行了改进。

Unit 2 Living with AI

（2）名词转换成形容词

This particular case highlighted the absolute necessity of taking climate change adaptation measures in transport to support trade and development.	这一特例强调，为支持贸易和发展，在运输方面采取适应气候变化的措施是绝对有必要的。
The grinder is used for making precision tooling.	这台研磨机用于制作精细的工具。

4. 转换成汉语副词

（1）形容词转换成副词

Organic light-emitting diodes (OLEDs) have found wide applications in high-resolution, large-area televisions and the handheld displays of smartphones and tablets.	有机发光二极管已广泛应用于高分辨率、大屏幕电视以及智能手机和平板电脑的手持显示器中。
They considered that the public might be receptive to a slight adjustment in the polling hours.	他们认为，公众或许会接受对投票时间稍作调整。

（2）名词转换成副词

The United Nations was applauded with the instinct to reject a business-as-usual approach in these dire circumstances.	在严峻局势下，联合国本能拒绝采用常规操作，这种做法受到赞许。

（3）动词转换成副词

In the final stages of fighting poverty, China succeeded in raising all the rural poor out of extreme poverty and the impoverished areas achieved a big stride in economic and social development, taking on a brand-new look.	在脱贫攻坚的最后阶段，中国成功地使农村贫困人口全部脱贫。贫困地区的经济和社会发展向前迈出了一大步，面貌焕然一新。

→ Exercises

I. Translate the following terms into Chinese.

1. Internet of Things (IoT)

   _____

2. User Interface (UI)

   _____

3. cryptocurrency

4. nanochip

5. metauniverse

6. fog computing

7. Data Lake (DL)

8. quantum entanglement

9. carbon neutrality

10. Artificial Intelligence Generated Content (AIGC)

II. Translate the following sentences into Chinese. Use the method of conversion to translate the underlined parts.

1. Days or weeks of sleeping in overly warm rooms can not only exacerbate chronic conditions like diabetes and heart disease, but also <u>negatively affect</u> psychiatric disorders, suicide risk, memory, mood and cognitive function.

2. Thinness was <u>fashionable</u> in the 19th century, when it was thought that "if you looked too robust, you looked like a working woman".

3. This sinking effect, or "overturning", allows the currents to transfer enormous amounts of heat around the planet, making them hugely influential for the climate around the Atlantic and beyond.

4. Rigorous evaluation of educational programs and policies is necessary to assess their effectiveness in improving student outcomes, identifying areas for improvement, and informing future decision-making in the field of education.

Unit 3

Advanced Materials, Advanced Life

Part I
Reading

What Is Smart Clothing Technology and How Does It Work?

Maia Mulko

① Modern fabric technology includes the intelligent modification of clothes to produce a determined effect. Clothes can be re-designed with the aid of technology to change colors, block sunlight, collect medical data, emit *vibrations*, or even display custom messages. Here are some of the most amazing advancements in fabric technology and smart fabrics.

Self-Cleaning Clothes

② Back in 2016, scientists at the Royal Melbourne Institute of Technology, in Australia, developed a self-cleaning fabric by "growing" copper and silver *nanostructures* on the cotton fibers of a piece of cloth. The process of getting the metal nanostructures onto the *textile* involved *priming* the cotton fabric using an acidic *solution* of tin chloride, then dipping the fabric into a *palladium* salt solution, causing palladium (a rare metal) nuclei to spontaneously form on the fibers. Finally, copper and silver baths led to the growth of *photoactive* metal nanostructures.

③ The metal atoms of these nanostructures get excited with light. When exposed to light, the material is able to break down organic matter, cleaning itself of stains and *grime* in less than six minutes.

④ The invention may be useful in *catalysis*-based industries, such as *agrochemicals* and *pharmaceuticals*, but there is still more work to do to improve the technique and especially, to try and ensure that metal nanoparticles are not released into the wastewater (if the clothes are actually washed), leading to environmental issues.

⑤ Silver nanoparticles have also been used to prevent odors by killing bacteria, but they can become toxic ions under certain conditions.

Fabrics That Cool You Down

⑥ Using air conditioners and electric fans to cool down accounts for nearly 20% of the total consumption of electricity used in buildings. So what if people could avoid heating up in the first place?

⑦ In 2020, a team of researchers from Stanford University (USA) and Nanjing University (China) modified a few pieces of silk—a fabric that already feels cool over human skin because it reflects much of the sunlight that strikes it—to make it reflect up to 95% of sunlight. This way, they managed the silk to stay 3.5°C cooler than the surrounding air in the sunlight.

⑧ The scientists achieved this by adding aluminum oxide nanoparticles to the silk fibers. These nanoparticles are able to reflect the ultraviolet wavelengths of sunlight and it proved so by keeping skin about 12.5°C cooler than cotton clothing.

⑨ First, the scientists used simulated skin made from silicone skin to test the product. When they *draped* the engineered silk over the simulated skin, it kept the skin 8°C cooler under direct sunlight than natural silk.

⑩ Then, they made a long-sleeved shirt from the engineered silk and asked a volunteer to wear it while standing out in the sun on a 37°C day. By analyzing *infrared* images, the researchers found out that the modified silk did not warm up as much as natural silk or cotton textiles.

⑪ More than a year earlier, a team of researchers from the University of Manchester's National *Graphene* Institute designed new smart textiles for heat *adaptative* clothing by taking advantage of the infrared *emissivity* (the ability to radiate energy) of graphene.

⑫ "Ability to control the thermal radiation is a key necessity for several critical applications such as temperature management of the body in excessive temperature climates. Thermal blankets are a common example used for this purpose. However, maintaining these functionalities as the surroundings heats up or cools down has been an outstanding challenge," said the leader of the research, Professor Coskun Kocabas, at the time.

Energy-Harvesting Clothes

⑬ In 2016, researchers from the Georgia Institute of Technology in Atlanta created a fabric that harvests energy from both sunlight and motion. To make the fabric, the team wove together *strands* of wool, solar cells constructed from lightweight polymer fibers with fiber-based triboelectric nanogenerators, which generate a small amount of electrical power from mechanical motion such as rotation, sliding, or vibration.

⑭ The fabric is 320 micrometers thick and is highly flexible, breathable, and lightweight. The team *envisions* it could one day be integrated into tents, curtains, or even clothing. One day, this technology could even help us charge our phones on the go.

⑮ "The objective was to harvest energy from our living environment. The goal is to drive small electronics," said Zhonglin Wang, one of the nanotechnologists authoring the investigation. "And this research recently attracted a lot of attention because these days, flexible electronics, wearable electronics, have become very popular and fashionable. But each of them needs a power source."

Programmable Fibers

⑯ In June 2021, engineers at the Massachusetts Institute of Technology developed "*programmable* fibers" that could let us carry data in our clothes. The fibers are made of silicon chips that are electrically connected to each other. This way, they can have a certain file storage capacity that can last up to two months without extra power.

⑰ According to senior researcher Yeol Fink, these digital fibers could also act as sensors to monitor physical performance and possibly even detect diseases, especially if they integrate a neural network. A neural network can help predict the user's activity and body patterns and eventually produce the early detection of a *respiratory* or a health problem.

Biometrics Monitoring Clothes

⑱ Fitness watches are not the only wearable devices that can monitor your activity, heart rate, sleep habits, etc. There are also activewear, workwear, sleepwear, and even underwear that do that through sensors. Linking with an app, the underwear created by the award-winning smart textile company Myant measures stress levels, stationary time, and other common options for wearable devices, as well as *ovulation* and driver fatigue.

⑲ In 2020, MIT researchers also created a washable sensor that monitors the vital signs of the wearer and has the potential of becoming the next big revolution in the remote healthcare field. Meanwhile, the Empa research center in Switzerland has integrated optic fibers into smart textiles to control the skin's circulation to avoid bed sores for immobile patients.

⑳ On the other hand, Danish company Edema ApS created washable stockings modified to detect changes in leg volume, which is especially useful for patients suffering from fluid accumulation or potential blood *clots* in that part of the body.

㉑ As you can see, there are several applications for smart clothing, and many others are expected to appear anytime soon. And while smart clothes may not be mainstream yet, they may someday *revolutionize* the way we dress, one way or another.

→ Words and Expressions

vibration *n.* a continuous slight shaking movement 震动；颤动

nanostructure *n.* an extremely small structure such as a semiconductor or optoelectronic device with dimensions of 0.1 nm–50 nm 纳米结构

textile *n.* any type of cloth made by weaving or knitting 纺织品

prime *vt.* to put a special layer of paint on a surface, in order to prepare it for the next layer 给（表面）涂上底漆

solution *n.* a liquid in which something is dissolved 溶液

palladium *n.* a soft silver-white metal that is often combined with gold and silver, and used to cover an object with a very thin layer of metal [化学] 钯

photoactive *adj.* capable of responding to light or other electromagnetic radiation 光敏的；感光性的

grime *n.* dirt that forms a layer on the surface of something 尘垢；污点

catalysis *n.* the process of making a chemical reaction quicker by adding a catalyst 催化作用；刺激作用

agrochemical *n.* any chemical used in farming, especially for killing insects or for making plants grow better 农用化学品

pharmaceutical *n.* drugs and medicines 药物

drape *vt.* to cover or decorate somebody/something with material 覆盖；遮盖

infrared *adj.* having or using electromagnetic waves that are longer than those of red light in the spectrum, and that cannot be seen 红外线的

adaptative *adj.* having a capacity for adaptation 可适应的

emissivity *n.* a measure of the ability of a surface to radiate energy 发射率；发（放、辐）射能力

graphene *n.* a very strong, light form of carbon 石墨烯

strand *n.* a single thin piece of thread, wire, hair, etc.（线、绳、毛发等的）股；缕

envision *vt.* to imagine what a situation will be like in the future, especially a situation you intend to work towards 展望；想象

programmable *adj.* able to be controlled by a computer or an electronic program（计算机或电器）程控的

respiratory *adj.* relating to breathing or your lungs 呼吸的

ovulation *n.* the process of producing an egg (called an ovum) from the ovary 排卵；产卵作用

clot *n.* a thick almost solid mass formed when blood or milk dries 血块

revolutionize *vt.* to completely change the way people do something or think about something 使发生革命性巨变；使彻底变革

→ Notes

1. **Royal Melbourne Institute of Technology** 皇家墨尔本理工大学
   澳大利亚的一所世界知名综合型公立大学，位于维多利亚州的墨尔本市，成立于1887年。20世纪60年代，伊丽莎白二世女王为了表彰学校在"二战"期间所做出的贡献，正式授予学校"皇家"头衔，同时辅以皇家基金来支持学校的建设。

2. **University of Manchester's National Graphene Institute** 曼彻斯特大学国家石墨烯研究所
   当前英国乃至世界石墨烯相关研究的策源地，主要致力于开拓二维材料科学与应用前沿领域，同时兼顾石墨烯以及二维材料的产业化和商业化。

Unit 3 Advanced Materials, Advanced Life

3. **Georgia Institute of Technology in Atlanta** 亚特兰大佐治亚理工学院

   成立于 1885 年，是一所坐落于佐治亚州首府亚特兰大的公立研究型大学。与麻省理工学院、加州理工学院并称为美国三大理工学院，是美国南部最好的理工类院校之一。

4. **Myant** 迈恩特纺织计算公司

   设计、开发和生产可穿戴技术的研发中心，致力于开发改变人们生活的互联纺织品。其明星产品 Skiin 智能服装系列，内嵌传感器，可以监测穿戴者的心率、呼吸率、温度、运动、姿势和睡眠等生物特征。

5. **Edema ApS**

   ApS 为 "Anpartsselskab"（Danish term for a limited liability company）的缩写，指丹麦有限责任公司。该公司主营医疗和生物测量设备及其相关业务，其开发的一款可水洗长袜能让医生通过测量患者腿部体积的变化来确定他们是否患有水肿。

→ Reading Skills

Making Connections

Making connections while reading is to create a link between what is being read and what is already known. It is an effective reading strategy which can not only help readers better understand a text and remember important information, but also make them actively engaged during reading activities.

There are mainly three types of connections:

• text-to-self connections (the easiest type);

• text-to-text connections;

• text-to-world connections (the most challenging type).

(1) Text-to-self connections

The easiest connections readers can make are text-to-self connections. They are the links established between a particular text and the readers' personal experiences. Those with a wide range of experiences will often be able to make insightful and complex connections. Take this text about smart clothing technology for example. By relating the text message to your prior knowledge of fabrics, cloths, and fibers, you can create a text-to-self connection. In Paras. 7 and 8, the author mentions that silk reflects sunlight, and the addition of some nanoparticles to the silk can block more sunlight, resulting in cooler skin. If you activate your knowledge of silk fabrics and first-hand experience with silk clothes while reading these two paragraphs, you will have a more meaningful and memorable reading experience.

(2) Text-to-text connections

These connections occur when a text being read reminds the readers of other texts, such as articles or books by the same author, stories from a similar genre, or articles on the same topic. Text-to-text connection, also known as intertextuality, is a valuable skill for readers to possess. When connections occur between two texts on the same topic, readers can analyze and evaluate their similarities and differences. Such a comparison and exploration could help readers think critically about the topic from different perspectives and thus develop a more comprehensive understanding of the ideas presented. When you read this text, for example, the news or journal articles you previously read regarding smart clothing technology may offer important background information for you to understand the text, or provide additional knowledge you need to form rational judgements on the topic.

(3) Text-to-world connections

Text-to-world connections are created when readers use information from the world to understand a text. To make these connections, readers could relate the text to real-life events, concerns of society, or major social and economic issues. In this text, the author introduces the advancements in smart clothing technology and explains how it works. To probe deeper into the topic, you need to find out the technological factors that drive the development of smart clothing. You may also relate the text discussion to smart clothing products already available in the market and think about the reasons for the popularity of smart clothing as well as its influence on people's lives in recent years.

In conclusion, readers can engage in deeper and more critical thinking by making connections. These connections enable a wider context to be established, thereby making it easier for readers to understand the underlying themes, ideas, and messages in a text.

→ Exercises

I. Building Vocabulary

Choose the best word in the box to fill in each blank. Use each word only once and make proper changes where necessary.

revolutionize	envision	infrared	vibration	programmable
adaptative	emissivity	respiratory	solution	drape

1. The _____ sensors on the bowl detect movement and open the lid as your pet approaches.

2. As a friend, I have no problem interacting with any nationality that comes from a different culture, but as a life partner, I am not too sure how _____ I am.

3. Smoking places you at serious risk of cardiovascular and _____ disease.

4. Energy-efficient windows have an insulating glass unit, low _____ coatings, gas fill, and other engineering advancements that stop heat transfer.

5. The earthquake sent the _____ to a village a hundred miles away.

6. They _____ an equal society, free of poverty and disease.

7. The outfits are characterized by loose, flowing robes that _____ around the body, with sleeves that hang down to the knees.

8. It can be prescribed in tablet form or as an oral _____, eye drops, or ear drops.

9. This state-of-the-art theater includes a(n) _____ lighting system, movable sound shell and a balcony.

10. As we move into the future, 3D printing will _____ the way we shop, the way we manufacture and the way we treat sick people.

II. Understanding the Text

Think about the following questions while reading the text.

Text-to-self connections:

1. What do smart fabrics in the text remind you of?

2. How do you feel when you learn about smart clothes?

3. Do you have any smart clothes? If so, what are they? If not, do you want to buy some? What are the merits and demerits of smart clothes?

Text-to-text connections:

4. Have you ever read similar texts about fabric technology? Search for the information about fabric technology from books, newspapers or websites and check how it is similar to, or different from, what is mentioned in the text.

Text-to-world connections:

5. What are the factors driving the development of smart clothing?

6. What influence may smart clothing have on people's minds and ways of dressing?

III. Theme Exploration

The writer mentioned in the last paragraph, "... there are several applications for smart clothing, and many others are expected to appear anytime soon. And while smart clothes may not be mainstream yet, they may someday revolutionize the way we dress, one way or another." Although smart clothing has already been around for some years, particularly in the fields of fitness and healthcare, it takes time to go mainstream. Work in groups and discuss the opportunities and challenges faced by smart clothing technologies.

IV. Real-Life Project

Smart clothes are traditional clothing items that incorporate modern technology. Smart clothing and wearable technology tend to have good prospects in textile, military, entertainment, anti-counterfeiting, and other fields. More recent examples of smart clothing are utilizing even newer technologies to achieve a greater array of functions. In addition to smart clothing applications mentioned in the text, do you know of any other smart clothing items in the market? Please search for relevant information and make a three-minute presentation on one or two smart clothing items.

Part II
Writing

Title, Affiliation, and Acknowledgements

1. Title

The title is a small but important part of a research paper. It reflects the central message of a study and is usually a good starting point for potential readers. A well-written title not only facilitates indexing and makes a paper noticed, but also decides whether the paper is worth reading or not.

1) Features of a Good Research Paper Title

A good research paper title has some well-mentioned characteristics.

First, it contains keywords that will make a paper recognizable to search engines.

Second, it is specific and informative. For example, the title "Hybrid Deep Learning-based Models for Crop Yield Prediction" clearly shows the research method, subject, and scope of the study. To avoid the risk of confusion, a good title is also cautious with the use of jargon and non-standard abbreviations.

Third, it is concise. Brevity is one feature mentioned in many style guides. The *Publication Manual of the American Psychological Association (APA)*, for example, suggests avoiding "words that serve no purpose" in research paper titles.

2) Capitalization of Research Paper Titles

There are no fixed rules for the capitalization of research paper titles. For most writers, the choice is between two major capitalization styles (title case and sentence case) according to the formatting requirements of specific journals. In title case (up style), all words are capitalized except for articles, conjunctions, and short prepositions, while in sentence case (down style), the title is written in the form of a sentence, in which the first letter of the first word, the first letter of any proper noun, and all letters of acronyms are capitalized.

Styles	Examples
title case	A Multiple Random Feature Extraction Algorithm for Image Object Tracking
sentence case	Decisional DNA based intelligent knowledge model for flexible manufacturing system

3) Structure of Research Paper Titles

Nominal structure and compound structure are frequently used to construct research paper titles.

• **Nominal structure:** Titles of this type are composed of nouns or noun phrases qualified by pre- modifiers and/or post-modifiers. For example:

[1] Reliability Evaluation of Renewable Energy Share in Power Systems

[2] The Lexical Sophistication of Second Language Learners' Academic Essays

• **Compound structure:** Most compound titles consist of two parts—title and subtitle—separated by a colon. This structure enables authors to pack more information into their titles, with the first part indicating the topic or subject and the second part presenting the method, scope, or description of the research, as shown in the following examples:

[3] Critical Review of the Use of Reference Electrodes in Li-Ion Batteries: A Diagnostic Perspective

[4] Art Technology Integration: Digital Storytelling as a Transformative Pedagogy in Primary Education

2. Author Affiliation

In research papers, author affiliation refers to the school, university, or institution to which the author belongs. It is a very necessary part because it gives credibility to a paper and implies responsibility and accountability for the published work. The affiliation of a paper is often placed below the author's name. In collaborative research, papers usually have multiple affiliations. Different authors may be associated with one institution or different institutions, and one author may also have several affiliations. The affiliation information, including institution name, city and post code, as well as country, is generally arranged from the smallest to the largest units. Sometimes the author's e-mail address might also be included. The following two examples show the typical sequence in which affiliation information is listed:

[5] International Center for Quantum Materials, School of Physics, Peking University, Beijing 100871, P. R. China.

[6] Centre for Microscopy and Microanalysis and School of Engineering, The University of Queensland, Queensland 4072, Australia.

3. Acknowledgements

The acknowledgements section often comes at the end of a research paper to signal the closure of the paper, but in some papers, it also appears at the bottom of the first page. Hyland (2018) regarded acknowledgements as a way of establishing research credibility and acknowledging the contributions of individuals or institutions. Unlike thesis or dissertation acknowledgements, acknowledgements in research papers often take the form of a single and short paragraph. The most common elements include appreciation for financial support and appreciation for individual intellectual or technical help. As for writing style, although it is appropriate to express gratitude in the first-person pronoun "I" or "we", acknowledgements in research papers are mostly formal. Some researchers use "the author(s)" as the grammatical subject of thanks to avoid personal pronouns, as illustrated in Example [8].

[7] We acknowledge the financial support from Australian Research Council through its DP programs. The financial support from the National Natural Science Foundation of

China (nos. 51629201, 51825204) and the Key Research Program of Frontier Sciences CAS (QYZDBSSW-JSC039) is also appreciated. (financial support)

[8] The authors are thankful to the anonymous reviewers for valuable comments and suggestions (intellectual help). This research was supported by the Bulgarian National Fund of Science under Project I02/20–2014. (financial support)

→ Exercises

I. Improve the following titles.

1. A Study of the Effects of Transformed Letters on Reading Speed

2. Design and Develop a Blockchain-Based Secure Scoring Mechanism for Online Learning

3. The Trends and Perspectives of Global Pandemic and Digital Marketing

4. Exploring the Influence of IP on Cultural Creative Art Design from the Perspective of Cultural Sociology

5. An Application Study of Mean Shift Algorithm in Image Segmentation

II. What are the criteria for a good research paper title? What are the linguistic features of English research paper titles? Find some English research paper titles from journals in your discipline and analyze the features of the titles.

III. Check the English journals in your discipline for any acknowledgements. Imitate them and write the acknowledgements section for your paper.

Unit 3 Advanced Materials, Advanced Life

学术论文标题翻译

一、学术论文标题特征

1. 标题内容要素

从内容上看，有些汉语学术论文标题只呈现研究对象和研究问题两个基本要素，有些则包含研究对象、研究问题、研究方法、研究环境或条件等多个要素。例如：

[1] <u>变刚度柔性夹持装置</u>（研究对象）的<u>研究进展</u>（研究问题）

[2] <u>人力资源</u>（研究对象）<u>在资产负债表中</u>（研究环境）的<u>确认与计量</u>（研究问题）

[3] 从<u>学习进化的视角</u>（研究方法）看 <u>ChatGPT/ 生成式人工智能</u>（研究对象）对<u>学习的影响</u>（研究问题）

2. 标题结构特点

并列式和偏正式是汉语学术论文标题的主要结构类型。并列式结构是由两个并列的名词或名词词组组成；偏正式结构一般由多个修饰语加中心名词组成。

[4] <u>中国种植业面源污染的</u>（修饰语）<u>区域差异</u>（中心名词）<u>及其</u>（并列连词）<u>脱钩效应</u>（中心名词）

[5] <u>粉末粒度</u>（修饰语）对<u>钛合金闭式叶轮成形</u>（修饰语）的<u>影响</u>（中心名词）

二、学术论文标题翻译方法

1. 正确使用名词结构

英语学术论文标题一般由名词性短语（包括动名词短语）构成，其中"名词（名词短语）+ 介词（分词 / 不定式）短语"是最常见的结构，因此把汉语标题翻译成英语时，一般不使用句子或动词短语。例如：

| 基于政府补贴的创业投资定价与决策 | Pricing and Decision Making of Venture Capital Based on Funding Policies |

太赫兹技术在农产品品质检测中的研究进展	Research Progress of Terahertz Technique in Quality Inspection of Agro-Food Products

2. 合理安排中心词和修饰语

  汉语学术论文标题中的修饰词往往较多，且一般出现在中心名词前面，而英语标题里中心名词的修饰语既可以前置也可以后置，后置修饰语一般由介词短语、分词短语、不定式等充当。英译时一般先厘清汉语标题的内容要素，找到中心名词，随后根据修饰语的功能，借助介词或连词合理安排修饰语的位置。例如：

个人金融数据的（修饰语）敏感性识别（中心名词）与隐私计量（中心名词）研究	Sensitivity Identification and Privacy Measurement of Personal Financial Data
免疫学的（修饰语）发展（中心名词）及其对医学的（修饰语）影响（中心名词）	Development of Immunology and Its Effect on Medical Science

3. 注意英汉差异省略冗词

  汉语学术论文标题特别是人文学科论文标题中常出现"关于……""论……""……刍议""漫谈……""……初探"等词语，由于这些表达并没有实际具体的意义，英译时可省略不译。例如：

我国塑料碳排放核算体系搭建与应用初探	The Construction and Application of China's Plastic Carbon Emission Accounting System
术语命名理念与策略的更新刍议——以"元宇宙"为例	New Mindset and Strategies of Terminology Naming: A Case Study of Metaverse
漫谈冰球大力击射中的力学原理	Mechanical Principle of Slap Shot in Ice Hockey

4. 巧妙利用副标题

  英译汉语学术论文标题时也可采用复合式结构，即借助副标题来化解翻译中的结构处理难题，使标题更简练，同时凸显重点信息。例如：

关于计算机软件程序漏洞的实时检测仿真	Real Time Detection of Computer Software Program Vulnerabilities: A Simulation Study（表明研究方法）
社会文化理论视角下的高校英语教师学习研究	An Investigation into College English Teacher Learning: A Sociocultural Perspective（表明理论视角）

5. 灵活运用常用标题结构

汉语学术论文标题中会出现一些相似的结构模式，我们可结合学科方向进行整理并在翻译中灵活运用。以下是一些常见标题结构及示例：

常用结构	举例
基于 A 的……研究 research of... based on A / ...based research of...	基于知识模型的接触网缺陷智能视觉辨识 Knowledge Model Based Intelligent Visual Identification of Catenary Defects
A 在 B 中的应用 application of A in B	现代艺术设计中抽象艺术语言的应用 Application of Abstract Art Language in Modern Art Design
A 对 B 的影响 effect/influence of A on B	间断供电对污泥电脱水效果的影响 Effect of Intermittent Power Supply on Sludge Electro-Dewatering
A 在……方面的进展 advances/progress of A in...	分子印迹技术在生命科学研究中的进展 Research Progress of Molecular Imprinting Technology in the Life Science
……视角下的…… ... from the perspective of...	复杂动态系统理论视角下二语写作发展的变异性研究 Variability in L2 Writing Development from the Perspective of Complex Dynamic Systems Theory

→ Exercises

Translate the following titles into English.

1. 基于深度学习的跨社交网络用户匹配方法

2. 论我国《著作权法》立法宗旨的修改——以促进文化产业发展为视角

3. 多维互动模式对二语词汇习得的影响

4. 可解释深度学习在光谱和医学影像分析中的应用

5. AI生成与学者撰写中文论文摘要的检测与差异性比较研究——以图书馆学领域为例

Unit 4

New Energy, New Future

Part I
Reading

Technology: Powering the Future of Energy

Byjon Heggie

① Deep in the sun's core, two **protons** of hydrogen atoms **collide** violently. Under immense pressure they **fuse** together and release vast amounts of energy in a process known as nuclear fusion. Travelling at the speed of light, some of this solar energy reaches Earth, where it powers our planet. From kettles to cars, almost all of the energy that we rely on originates from the sun: Fossil fuels were once plants energized by **photosynthesis**; solar panels absorb sunlight and convert it into electricity; even windfarms and hydroelectric power stations rely on the sun's energy to warm the land and sea to create the wind and rain-fed rivers that turn their **turbines**. To power our increasingly electrified lives, there is an abundance of clean and renewable energy sources that we can draw on. And technology is at the **cutting edge** of **harnessing** this renewable energy more efficiently.

② Solar panels are one of the most **ubiquitous** renewable energies, already generating more than 3.5 percent of the world's electricity. But there is scope for improvement: Capturing just one hour of the world's sunlight would power the planet for a year. Not only are more solar panels being installed, but technology is also finding ways to make them more efficient. Placing **hexagonal** lenses into a panel's protective glass **coating**, for example, can concentrate the incoming light to achieve an efficiency rate of about 30 percent, compared to an industry standard of 15–22 percent. Adding thin layers of silicon to both sides of a solar cell increases its efficiency to around 25 percent.

③ However, with silicon, one of the most energy intensive components of traditional solar panels, science has developed an alternative using **perovskite** crystals. These can be made both transparent and flexible, bringing the possibility of photovoltaic building materials such as windows and roof *tiles,* and even wearable fabrics. Another big advance has been PERC (Passivated Emitter Rear Cell) technology that reflects unabsorbed light back into the solar cell for a second chance at conversion into electricity. PERC also enables solar panels to be *bifacial*—capturing sunlight on both sides with sun-tracking technology moving the panel to ensure maximum exposure.

④ Among the most recognizable forms of renewable energy is wind power, with wind turbines an increasingly common feature of both landscapes and coastlines. Wind already generates more than six percent of global electricity, and technologies are being developed that will make wind turbines cheaper, more efficient, and more powerful. A key focus has been on the *blades* that catch the wind's *kinetic* energy, with technological improvements, including 3D printing, enabling blades to be built longer and lighter for greater efficiency. Research has also added a gently curved tip to the blade that helps it make the most of even light winds, and smart blades that can adjust themselves to the wind flow for peak performance.

⑤ Computer modelling of the complex physics of wind flow not only determines the best locations for wind power, but the precise *configuration* of wind turbines to maximize the wind they catch as it flows through the farm. Wind *deflecting* turbines have even been developed that divert the wind hitting the tower onto the blades so that even more energy is harnessed. Beyond this, future developments being explored include Airborne Wind Energy that operates like a kite, the absence of a tower making it cheaper to *deploy* and able to reach higher altitudes where winds are often stronger.

⑥ By far the biggest producer of renewable energy is hydropower, with running water generating around 17 percent of the world's electricity. Despite having more than a century of experience behind it, hydropower technology is still making improvements. One of the biggest opportunities is with low head hydropower that can generate electricity from even a gentle slope. The development of an Archimedes Hydrodynamic Screw system, where the water flows down the screw, turning it as it descends, has shown how effectively low head hydropower can be deployed for widespread, small-scale hydropower generation.

⑦ The use of technology to gather and analyze data is also improving efficiency: Many hydroelectricity plants are decades old, so evaluating details of their ***deterioration*** can ***proactively preempt*** problems. Even more, analytical tools such as ***hydrological*** forecasting, seasonal hydro-systems analysis, day-ahead scheduling, and real-time operations are helping hydro plants operate more efficiently. This becomes even more important with climate change bringing more variable and extreme water flows, for which high-tech weather forecasting will be crucial.

⑧ With all this energy originating from the sun, scientists are working to imitate the sun's nuclear fusion on Earth. Long considered the stuff of science fiction, the reality of nuclear fusion providing safe, abundant energy on Earth is increasingly a question of "when" not "if". One project working to demonstrate the feasibility of nuclear fusion is ITER, the International Thermonuclear Experimental Reactor. Taking on one of the biggest technical and technological challenges ever faced, the ITER project brings together scientists from around the world to build the world's largest machine of its kind, the ITER Tokamak. This is where hydrogen ***isotopes*** will be heated to 150 million degrees Celsius, theoretically fusing together to release 10 times more energy than they take in. With more than one million components and 10 million parts, technology is key to a project of this scale. And technology services company Capgemini has been working with ITER for years.

⑨ Capgemini partners with companies and organizations to transform their activities by harnessing the power of technology. Working with ITER, Capgemini has provided ***a raft of*** support for bringing its vision to life by combining engineering, technology, and project management expertise. From supporting the construction of technical buildings to applying advanced engineering expertise to make sure the visions of scientists and engineers are feasible, Capgemini has worked with ITER for more than a decade on bringing this ***unprecedented*** project to ***fruition***. It has also been developing the features for a digital twin—a precise digital copy of the proposed Tokamak. Bringing together all of the available data in a way that makes it accessible to everyone involved, the digital twin will allow every element to be tested, simulating the stages of construction and improving the design by identifying and resolving issues. By placing all the data in a single unified source, Capgemini will enable ITER to make more informed decisions and improve the project's overall efficiency and performance. The vision is for the digital twin to be a critical component of operationalizing this experiment for generations to come.

⑩ As the world looks to end its reliance on fossil fuels, the improvements being made in solar, wind, and hydro—along with the promise of nuclear fusion—are crucial to meeting the United Nation's Sustainable Development Goal of affordable, reliable, sustainable, and modern energy for all. We have the ability to generate carbon-free energy: The sun has provided the answer—and technology is helping to unlock it.

→ Words and Expressions

proton *n.* a very small piece of matter with a positive electrical charge that is in the central part of an atom 质子

collide *vi.* to hit something or someone that is moving in a different direction from you 碰撞；相撞

fuse *vi.* to join together physically, or to make things join together, and become a single thing 融合；熔接

photosynthesis *n.* the process by which green plants turn carbon dioxide and water into food using energy obtained from light from the sun 光合作用

turbine *n.* an engine or motor in which the pressure of a liquid or gas moves a special wheel around 涡轮机；汽轮机

cutting edge the newest, most advanced stage in the development of something（处于某事物发展的）尖端；最前沿

harness *vt.* to control and use the force or strength of something to produce power or to achieve something 控制；利用（以产生能量等）

ubiquitous *adj.* seeming to be everywhere or in several places at the same time; very common 无处不在的；十分普遍的

hexagonal *adj.* (of a flat shape) having six straight sides and six angles 六角形的；六边形的

coating *n.* a thin layer of something that covers a surface 涂层；（薄的）覆盖层

perovskite *n.* a mineral that contains various types of metals that are used in industry 钙钛矿

tile *n.* a thin curved piece of baked clay used for covering roofs（铺屋顶的）瓦

bifacial *adj.* having two faces or fronts 双面的

blade *n.* the flat wide part of an object that pushes against air or water 叶片；桨叶

kinetic *adj.* [usually before noun] of or produced by movement 运动的；运动引起的

configuration *n.* the shape or arrangement of the parts of something 布局；结构；构造

deflect *vt.* to change direction or make something change direction, especially after hitting something（使）偏斜；（使）转向

deploy *vt.* to organize and send out (people or things) to be used for a particular purpose 部署，调动

deterioration *n.* the fact or process of becoming worse 恶化；退化

proactively *adv.* in a way that involves controlling a situation by making things happen rather than waiting for things to happen and then reacting to them 主动地；有前瞻性地

preempt *vt.* to prevent something from happening by taking action to stop it 预先制止；防止

hydrological *adj.* relating to the study of water on the earth, for example, where it is and how it is used 水文的；水文学的

isotope *n.* one of the possible different forms of an atom of a particular element 同位素

a raft of a large amount or number of 许多

unprecedented *adj.* never having happened before, or never having happened so much 前所未有的；空前的

fruition *n.* the successful result of a plan, a process or an activity（计划、过程或活动的）完成；成果

➔ Notes

1. **nuclear fusion** 核聚变，核融合
   指两个轻原子核结合成一个较重的原子核并释放出巨大能量的过程。在可控条件下，核聚变可能成为未来的能量来源。

2. **PERC** (Passivated Emitter Rear Cell) 钝化发射区背面接触电池
   一种新型太阳能电池。该电池在传统电池的背面添加了介质钝化层，可大幅减少光电损失、增加光吸收概率。

3. **Airborne Wind Energy** 空中风能
   各种自主飞行设备的统称。这些设备可以飞到传统风力涡轮机无法企及的高空采集风能。例如，德国天帆电力公司（SkySails Power）开发的一种新型风力涡轮机可以像风筝一样捕捉高空风来发电。

4. **low head hydropower** 低水头水力发电
   水头指水流在垂直方向上的能量，常用于衡量水流的压力和速度的大小。水头越高，势能越大，同等流量可发电也越多。低水头水电站通常指水头在 40 米以下的水电站，多建于坡降平缓的中下游河段。

5. **Archimedes Hydrodynamic Screw** 阿基米德流体动力螺杆
   又称阿基米德螺杆，以古希腊哲学家、科学家、数学家阿基米德的名字命名，是最早的一种水力机械。阿基米德螺杆是一项具有革命性的发明，自古代起就运用于农田灌溉、矿井排水等多个领域，今天仍在水力发电行业中发挥作用。

6. **International Thermonuclear Experimental Reactor** 国际热核聚变实验堆计划
   ITER 计划是为解决人类未来能源问题而开展的国际科技合作计划。该计划集成了当今国际受控磁约束核聚变研究的主要科技成果，建造可实现大规模聚变反应的聚变实验堆。目前合作承担 ITER 计划的七个成员是欧盟、中国、韩国、俄罗斯、日本、印度和美国。

7. **Tokamak** 托卡马克装置
   一种利用磁约束来实现受控核聚变的环形容器。其名字来源于俄语的"环形"（toroidal）、"真空室"（kamera）、"磁"（magnit）和"线圈"（kotushka），最初由苏联阿齐莫维齐等人在 20 世纪 50 年代发明。该装置是目前实现可控核聚变的主流方式。

8. **Capgemini** 凯捷管理顾问公司
   全球知名管理咨询、技术和外包服务供应商。总部位于法国巴黎，由法国企业家 Serge Kampf 于 1967 年创立。

→ Reading Skills

Effective Reading and Note-Taking

Note-taking is the practice of creating a condensed and organized record of the key points of information from a source. The ability to take notes actively and effectively while reading is an important part of college academic success. It helps with reading comprehension and makes it easier for readers to master the essentials of reading materials.

Specifically speaking, good note-taking can help readers:

- Keep engaged while reading;
- Organize key ideas and information from the reading materials;
- Record and remember important concepts;
- Make connections between ideas regarding the reading topics;
- Review the major information points;
- Think critically about what is read.

There is no one right way to take notes while reading. It is a matter of choice and personal preference. What's important for readers is to find a format that works best for them or to switch between different formats depending on the reading purposes.

Here are some common formats for note-taking:

(1) Linear note-taking

It is also called sequential note-taking or outlining. Linear notes are written in a list-like format, which includes headings for the main ideas and subheadings for the supporting points. Numbering/lettering and indentation are often used to help organize the format.

(2) Diagrammatic note-taking

This format uses diagrams such as mind maps, concept maps, tables, flow charts, and timelines to organize key information visually and show connections between ideas.

(3) Cornell note-taking

To use this format, one needs to divide the page into two columns, with detailed notes in the right column and key words, reflections, cues or questions in the left column. Besides, there is usually a brief summary section at the bottom of the page, which prompts note-takers to formulate the gist of the information in their own words. Cornell note-taking helps readers develop critical thinking skills and review notes efficiently.

Here is an example of the Cornell format of notes on hydropower:

Questions	Notes
What is the current condition of hydropower?	The largest renewable energy producer; Running water generates about 17% of the world's electricity.
How does technology improve the hydropower efficiency?	**Technology 1**: development of an Archimedes Hydrodynamic Screw system **Benefit**: effective use of low head hydropower to generate electricity
	Technology 2: data gathering and analysis **Benefits**: evaluate decades-old hydroelectricity plants to preempt problems; analytical tools help hydro plants operate more efficiently.

Summary:
Although hydropower is one of the oldest sources of renewable energy, it still has room for improvement and opportunity for growth with the aid of technology.

Finally, here are some note-taking tips:

- Highlight key words or phrases;

- Use symbols and abbreviations;

- Use colors to mark different notes;

- Keep notes brief, focused, and well-organized;

- Take notes in your own words instead of copying from the text.

→ Exercises

I. Building Vocabulary

Choose the best word in the box to fill in each blank. Use each word only once and make proper changes where necessary.

| deploy | collide | proactively | unprecedented | configuration |
| harness | ubiquitous | deterioration | preempt | fruition |

1. Unlike fixed wind turbines, which can only operate in shallow waters, floating turbines can generate electricity further offshore, _____ the power of stronger ocean winds.

2. When multiple drones are working together in the same airspace, there's a risk that they might _____.

3. For those looking to budget and track expenses, mobile apps are a good idea because phones are _____ and make logging easy and quick.

4. The local branch of the Red Cross has _____ medical teams, emergency food, water supplies, and rescue helicopters.

5. The Global Development Initiative (GDI) has become a beacon of hope and a catalyst for international development cooperation in a world that has faced _____ challenges over recent years.

6. The technology provides constant monitoring, data analysis, and support to predict and _____ failure.

7. Hard work pays off, and our efforts over the past three years have come to _____.

8. It is an acknowledgment that businesses must _____ identify and address risks to ensure the stability and security of supply chains.

9. The Chinese space station features a basic three-module _____ consisting of the core module, Tianhe, and two lab modules, Wentian and Mengtian.

10. The mining of silica sand can cause significant environmental damage, ranging from land _____ to the loss of biodiversity.

II. Understanding the text

In this text, the author introduces how technology could be used to power the future of energy. Read the text again and write your notes for the four types of energy using one of the formats mentioned in the Reading Skills section (Linear, Diagrammatic, and Cornell).

III. Theme Exploration

From residential rooftops to utility-scale farms, solar energy is reshaping energy markets around the world and is likely to be deployed on a large scale in the future. Many countries are investing huge sums of money in harnessing solar energy. It looks promising not only for being a wise solution to the global energy shortage but also for providing clean energy to combat climate change. However, there are still challenges to realizing its full potential, such as storage and high cost, which limit its development and widespread application. Please work in pairs and discuss the application and challenges of solar energy. Provide examples to illustrate your ideas.

IV. Real-Life Project

In 2022, the International Energy Agency (IEA) published a report entitled "Tracking Clean Energy Innovation: Focus on China". According to the report, China has strengthened its position as an energy innovator on the global stage due to several decades of increasing policy focus on technology innovation. China has been committed to driving the energy revolution and developing high-quality energy to better serve economic and social progress. Please search for relevant information and make a five-minute presentation on China's efforts and achievements in carbon emission reduction and green energy innovation in the last decade.

Part II
Writing

Abstract and Keywords

1. Functions of Abstracts

An abstract is a short summary that highlights the key points of a research paper, so it is regarded as a mini-version of the paper. As a self-contained part, it is about one-paragraph long and is often written to give readers a quick overview of the research work. An abstract serves two main purposes: First, it facilitates indexing by acting as a tool for information retrieval when accessed by search engines; Second, it enables potential readers to assess the relevance of the paper concerned to their own research before they decide whether to read the paper or not.

2. Types of Abstracts

Abstracts are of different types. Due to different writing purposes, the moves (a move is a stretch of text with a specific communicative function) included in the abstracts may also be different. Before introducing these types, let us look at the functions each of the following structural moves can perform in abstract construction:

Moves	Functions
Background	Providing concise introductory information about a research topic; Describing the current state of relevant research and limitations in previous studies; Explaining research motivation and significance.
Purpose	Introducing the research rationale, objectives, intentions, or scope.
Methods	Explaining concisely the methodology, including research information such as materials, equipment, procedures, models, theories, key variables, instruments, sampling method, or data collection process.

(Continued)

Moves	Functions
Results	Highlighting the major research findings, such as test results, observation results, or correlation between variables.
Conclusion	Presenting the significance of the findings or arguments; Stating the theoretical or practical implications of the findings.

Based on the information they carry, abstracts are basically classified into two major types: descriptive abstracts and informative abstracts.

1) Descriptive Abstracts

Descriptive abstracts are also called indicative abstracts. This type of abstract is like an outline of the paper. It may indicate the background, purpose, methods, and/or scope of the paper, but it does not provide any specific information about the results and conclusion. Therefore, most descriptive abstracts are rather short, no more than 100 words. They are more often found in review papers and non-empirical papers. Here is an example:

❶Phishing is the fraudulent attempt to obtain sensitive information by disguising oneself as a trustworthy entity in digital communication. ❷It is a type of cyber attack often successful because users are not aware of their vulnerabilities or are unable to understand the risks.	❶-❷ Background
❸This article presents a systematic literature review conducted to draw a "big picture" of the most important research works performed on human factors and phishing.	❸ Purpose
❹The analysis of the retrieved publications, framed along the research questions addressed in the systematic literature review, helps in understanding how human factors should be considered to defend against phishing attacks.	❹ Significance of the paper
❺Future research directions are also highlighted.	❺ Scope of the paper

2) Informative Abstracts

The majority of abstracts are informative. They offer more details about the paper, so they are generally longer and more comprehensive than descriptive abstracts. A typical informative abstract follows a five-move structure. It informs the readers of all the essential points of the research paper by briefly summarizing the background, purpose, methods, results, and conclusion of the research. Look at the structural moves and their sequencing in the informative abstract on the next page:

❶The progress of onshore wind expansion varies globally, as often expressed by a country's installed capacity and capacity factor. ❷However, installed capacity and capacity factor do not allow conclusions about how effectively and efficiently countries use their spatially diverse wind potential. ❸It is unknown how far wind energy expansion is and whether the countries use the available potential in the best possible way. ❹Thus, this study aims to quantify and compare the wind potential use effectiveness and efficiency for the 40 countries with the highest installed capacity in 2021. ❺A global wind turbine site dataset and the wind farm potential index were used for estimating the suitability of current wind turbine sites. ❻The wind potential use efficiency was calculated by comparing the (1) distributions of the wind farm potential index at wind turbine sites with (2) distributions of the wind farm potential index of the countries as a whole by the Kolmogorov-Smirnov test statistic. ❼The capacity-to-suitable-area ratio defined the wind potential use effectiveness. ❽The results reveal that 81.9% of the global onshore wind turbine fleet operates at suitable sites. ❾Simultaneous occurrences of high effectiveness and efficiency are not given in any country: China, Brazil, and Italy use their wind potential more efficiently than many other countries. ❿The USA and India adequately consider the wind resource efficiency for wind turbine siting. ⓫Germany has the highest effectiveness despite low efficiency. ⓬The results reveal how critical it is to quantify the progress of wind energy expansion based on the effectiveness and efficiency, not only the installed capacity and capacity factor.	❶-❸ Background (Introducing the research topic and the research gap) ❹ Purpose (Goal of the present research) ❺-❼ Methods (Methods in the present research) ❽-⓫ Results (Major findings of the present research) ⓬ Conclusion (Implications of the present research)

It is worth noting that not all structural moves are obligatory. For example, in some informative abstracts, the research background is omitted, and the abstracts start with the research purposes. The structure and length of abstracts vary according to disciplines, types of papers, and the specific requirements of journals.

3. Verb Tenses in Abstracts

Several verb tenses can be found in an abstract, and which tense to use largely depends on the specific functions of each structural move. The tenses used in an abstract are related to those in the corresponding sections of the paper. There are some general suggestions for the use of verb tenses in abstract writing:

Moves	Functions	Tenses
Background	Stating general facts or concepts	Simple present tense
	Describing prior research	Simple past tense / Present perfect tense

(Continued)

Moves	Functions	Tenses
Purpose	Research-oriented purpose (*this study, this research*…)	Simple past tense / Simple present tense
	Paper-oriented purpose (*this paper, this article*…)	Simple present tense
Methods	Introducing experimental/survey procedures	Simple past tense
	Introducing models, analytical methods, algorithm, instruments, samples, theories	Simple present tense
Results	Reporting actual findings or results of observation	Simple past tense / Simple present tense
Conclusion	Stating a conclusion or implications or recommendations	Simple present tense / Modal auxiliaries

4. Features of Keywords

Keywords are words or phrases that capture the most important aspects of a research paper, such as terms closely related to the research topic, key methods, or experimental techniques. They are mainly used for indexing in databases and as search terms for readers, so keywords are also named "indexing terms". Well-chosen keywords can make papers more discoverable. In most cases, the number of keywords in a research paper ranges from three to five. They are usually nouns or noun phrases written in lowercase letters (except for proper nouns and abbreviations) and can be separated by a comma, semicolon, or larger space.

→ Exercises

I. The following abstract is from a paper titled "Designing Trust: The Formation of Employees' Trust in Conversational AI in the Digital Workplace". The sentences in this abstract are randomly arranged below. Please restore them to their original order.

   A. While previous research showed that systems' use critically depends on users' trust, little is known about the development of trust in AI technologies.

   B. To answer the research questions, we conducted an interpretive single case study of a global organization.

C. The COVID-19 pandemic accelerated the adoption and use of AI technologies to support the virtualization of the workplace.

D. This research focuses on an AI chatbot as a type of organizational AI system and asks how and why employees' trust towards an AI chatbot is formed and sustained.

E. It contributes to the information systems literature by demonstrating the critical importance of emotional and organizational trust in complementing cognitive trust, as well as the key design features that promote trust in AI chatbot use.

F. The study identifies three types of trust experienced by AI chatbot users—emotional, cognitive and organizational—and develops a framework of experiential and sustained trust formation.

II. Read the following abstract and answer the questions below.

Research article (RA) abstracts constitute an important genre in higher education. Previous research on the RA abstract has often combined abstracts from journals in the same discipline, with the view of revealing possible intra/inter-disciplinary, cross-linguistic, cross-cultural, etc. variations. The present study analyzed empirical RA abstracts from *TESOL Quarterly*, a well-recognized journal in Applied Linguistics, with the view of revealing their rhetorical structure and linguistic peculiarities. Hundred (100) empirical RA abstracts collected from the website of the journal constituted the data for the study. The data were analyzed, with attention to the move structure (kinds, frequency, and sequencing of moves) as well as the linguistic realization of moves. The study revealed that *TESOL Quarterly* empirical RA abstracts feature a five-move structure, with the Purpose and Product moves being obligatory and the Introduction, Method, and Conclusion moves being core moves. It was also revealed that the abstracts were characterized by nine move sequences, with the five-move sequence (M1>M2>M3>M4>M5) dominating. The study also revealed that each move was characterized by unique configurations of linguistic features, particularly tense, voice, and grammatical subject roles. This study contributes to scholarship on

RA abstracts. It also has implications for pedagogy and practice, and serves as a trigger for further studies.

1. What type of abstract is it?
2. What are the moves in the abstract? Underline the markers or expressions that help you identify the moves.
3. What tenses are used in the abstract?
4. What are the possible keywords of the paper?

III. Find some abstracts of academic papers from journals in your research field. Analyze the abstracts based on the following questions and report your findings to the class.

1. What type of abstract does each one represent?
2. What are the functions of each sentence? Identify the structural moves in the abstracts.
3. What verb tenses are used in each abstract?

Part III
Translating

学术论文摘要翻译

一、学术论文摘要结构

汉语学术论文摘要和英语学术论文摘要包含的语步（即体裁结构要素）基本相同，以常见的信息型摘要为例，两种学术论文摘要中一般都包括研究目的、研究方法、研究结果和研究结论，有些摘要中还出现研究背景。它们是论文要点的高度概括和浓缩，涵盖了论文的主要内容及基本观点。例如：

（研究背景）现代生活方式的转变使居民夜间户外活动不断丰富，建设高质量城市夜间户外环境已成为居民生活的重要需求。户外环境已被证实与人的情绪感知存在关联，但已有研究主要关注日间环境而较少聚焦夜间。（**研究方法**）基于计算机视觉技术，通过采集夜间户外环境的图像数据，结合公众的情绪感知评价，并利用空间自相关与空间回归分析方法（**研究目的**）探究情绪感知在夜间户外环境的空间分布特征及其影响因素。（**研究结果**）结果表明：1）夜间低维护的蓝绿空间能使人具有更强烈的恐惧感但焦虑感较弱，而高品质的绿色空间使人产生的恐惧感和焦虑感均较弱；高密度建筑区的户外环境往往令人感到不舒畅，低密度建筑区的户外环境则能使人感到较不恐惧、舒畅和放松；2）夜间户外环境要素如绿视率、天空可视率、拥挤度、围合度及视觉可步行性在不同类型户外环境中与情绪感知的相关性存在差异。（**研究结论**）本研究为如何快速、精准地测度夜间户外环境对情绪感知的影响提供了参考，有助于建设城市夜间户外环境，以提升居民生活质量和健康福祉。

二、学术论文摘要翻译方法

英汉学术论文摘要在语步上具有同一性，但由于受到语言体系的影响，两者在词汇、句法和篇章层面上体现出一定的差异性。因此，英译汉语学术论文摘要时，需注意以下几点：

1. 确定中心动词，合理安排其他成分

译者应当先找到汉语各分句的谓语动词，根据谓语动词确定句子的主语、宾语及其他修饰成分的位置。对比下面中英文例句中词语的位置变化：

防儿童开启包装（CRPs）非常重要，因为它可以阻止儿童接触潜在有害的产品。然而，盖子上的锁紧机构仍然存在可用性问题。本研究旨在评估包装设计、抓握技术和年龄对扭矩传递的影响。	Child-Resistant Packagings (CRPs) are important because they prevent children accessing potentially harmful products. However, the locking mechanism located on the caps still presents usability problems. The aim of this study was to evaluate the effects of packaging design, gripping technique and age on the transmission of torque.

2. 合理断句，拆译长句

当汉语句子冗长复杂、包含了多个分句时，可将长句译成几个单句，选择合适的动词作为各个分句的谓语，并为这些谓语选择合适的主语。

原位杂交（FISH）技术是检测恶性肿瘤细胞核酸序列的常用方法，在癌症的诊疗领域有广泛应用。	FISH is a commonly used technique for the identification of nucleic acid sequences in malignant tumor cells. It has found wide application in cancer diagnosis and treatment.
针对热再生氨基液流电池电堆系统，设计开发了一个包含传输延时的动态模型，研究了不同系统设计和运行条件对系统性能的影响。	A dynamic model with the transmission delay was designed and developed for the thermally-regenerative ammonia-based flow battery (TRAFB) stack system. This model was utilized to investigate the effects of various system designs and operating conditions on the system performance.

3. 合并短句，注意衔接

当几个汉语句子内容简短或者句子之间有明显的关联时，可以根据句子的逻辑联系，使用衔接手段把这几个句子合译成一个英语长句。这样可以使句子之间更紧凑，符合学术用语简洁的文体特征。

为实现 FISH 实验的全自动化，设计了一种全自动病理染色系统。该系统设置有多轴操纵臂、试剂加样器、载玻片、盖玻片夹具、辅助模块等。	To achieve complete automation of FISH experiments, a fully automated pathological staining system was designed, which was equipped with multi-axis manipulators, reagent samplers, slides, cover slide fixtures, and auxiliary modules.

4. 灵活选择时态和语态

时态、语态的选择也是英译学术论文摘要时常常需要考虑的问题。就时态而言，译者需根据时态在英文摘要不同语步的分布特点，为每个句子选择恰当的谓语动词形式。在语态选择上，主动语态能使句子的意义表达更直观，易于读者理解，但涉及研究方法、实验模型、概述研究过程等方面的内容时，汉语摘要中会出现较多无主句，英译这些句子时，被动语态则是更好的选择，因此翻译时具体使用何种语态要根据情境合理选用。例如：

本文探究新能源汽车动力电池回收利用与循环经济发展的联系，然后分析其回收利用途径。	This paper explores the relationship between the recycling and reuse of power batteries in new energy vehicles and the development of circular economy. It then analyzes the methods for their recycling and reuse.
使用标定球对手术器械进行标定，采用 Polaris Vega 光学追踪器实时追踪手术器械，建立手术器械与 Polaris Vega 光学追踪器之间的坐标转换关系。	The calibration ball was utilized to calibrate surgical instruments, and the Polaris Vega optical tracker was employed to track these instruments in real time. This process established the coordinate transformation relation between the surgical instruments and the Polaris Vega optical tracker.

5. 术语专业精准，巧用名词化结构

对汉语学术论文摘要中的术语进行英译时，应结合专业语境，充分考虑英文词汇或表达方式在专业范围内的适用性。例如，"冷凝器"常译为"condenser"而非"cooler"，"人机交互"常译为"human-computer interaction"而非"man-machine interaction"。另外，名词化结构在英语学术论文摘要中出现频率较高，一方面增加了行文的客观性和正式度，另一方面也能使行文更加紧凑。因此，在英译汉语学术论文摘要时，可根据句子组织和表达需要灵活使用名词化结构。例如：

构建优势互补的多能源系统是能源互联网发展的必经之路。	The construction of a multi-energy system with complementary advantages is the only pathway to the development of energy Internet.
利用虚拟现实平台为改善自闭症谱系障碍中常见的社交障碍提供了一种有效的治疗选择。	The use of a virtual reality platform offers an effective treatment option for improving social impairments commonly found in autism spectrum disorders.

→ Exercises

Translate the following sentences into English.

1. 集成创新（integrated innovation）是国际中文教育高质量发展的根本需要和长远需求，也是学科建设的迫切需要。

2. 针对脊柱微创手术（minimally invasive spine surgery）实际的临床导航需求，设计开发了一种基于增强现实的脊柱微创手术导航系统。

3. 为了探究家庭功能对大学生心理异常的影响，2021 年 3 月至 9 月，在上海市高校采取分层随机抽样方法选取 1287 名大学生进行匿名问卷调查。

4. 研究结果表明，研究生的学术动机、科研投入、导学关系、导师指导、学术环境等因素均对学术志趣有显著影响。

Unit 4　New Energy, New Future

5. ChatGPT 的应用同时也面临着伦理、技术、意识形态等多方面挑战，对此应清醒认识，辩证看待。

6. 本研究对于提高我国英语写作课堂的教学质量和人才培养质量具有一定的启示。

Unit 5

The Future Is Now

Part I
Reading

Generative Design Proves That "The Future Is Now" for Engineers

Trevor English

① Generative design takes an approach towards engineering that we've never seen before in the digital *realm*. It *replicates* an evolutionary approach to design, considering all of the necessary characteristics. Couple this with high-performance computing and the cloud, and you're left with capabilities that engineers never thought they would have.

② The way in which engineers design is being brought into question with new generative design tools. If you're an engineer and haven't seen your workflows altered yet, prepare for the coming future.

③ The *onset* of practical artificial intelligence *algorithms* has enabled the possibility of mainstream generative design tools. That means engineers can create thousands of design options *inherent* to their digital design and choose which design meets their needs to the fullest. From here, you can solve *manufacturability* constraints and ultimately build better products.

④ If you've been in the CAD and engineering design space for any period of time, you know that generative design has long been a *buzzword* of the industry. Companies like Under Armour, Airbus, Black & Decker, and other massive corporations are embracing generative design as a trend shaping the future of the engineering industry. It allows engineers to hand the *reins* off to their CAD software to organically find the best solutions to a given set of constraints. It *augments* the engineer's imagination.

⑤ Through generative design, collaboration with technology can be organic and flowing. It results in ideas that are better than what you could come up with on your own, and products that are lighter and accomplish their directives better. It simply results in better engineers.

⑥ With all of that said, let's escape the showy buzz around the tech and see what's really possible.

What Can It Do?

⑦ Generative design is a tool that uses machine learning to **mimic** a design approach similar to nature. It **interfaces** with engineers by allowing input design **parameters** to problem-solving. If you have loads in certain locations, you need to maintain certain material thicknesses, or even keep certain costs, all that can be fed into generative design tools.

⑧ After you press run and let the algorithms do their thing, you're left with generative designs that meet your input criteria. From there, you can cycle through, pick which design is the most optimized for your design end goals, and modify from there. In essence, it takes you down a digital shortcut to **optimizing** the perfect design.

⑨ The advantages of generative design become apparent when you consider just what it takes to get started with any design. You approach problems with a general understanding of what your design needs to do, but you're left to your own creative devices to find a solution. Instead of starting a design based on the idea you have in your mind, you can start by offloading that data into a computer and allowing it to **kickstart** the design process.

⑩ One of the best examples of how this methodology and thus generative workflows can be practically implemented is by examining how to build a chair. Instead of starting with some sketches, creating various designs, and picking the best one, you can start by feeding a computer some constraints. Input the cost, the weight it needs to support, and what material you'd like your chair made out of. Then the computer can deliver thousands of design options that take into account manufacturability for you to select from. This is what generative design offers to the modern engineer.

Refining Generative Further

⑪ True generative design is software that uses the power of cloud computing and true machine learning to provide sets of solutions to the engineer. This is in **stark** contrast to tools we've seen before, such as topology optimization, latticing, or other similar CAD tools. All of these previous tools improve existing designs, whereas generative creates a new design.

⑫ Generative design is also different from other existing CAD tools in that it can consider manufacturability. If you've ever used tools like topology optimization or other fancy "generative" tools, you've probably been left with an end product that looks cool on paper but isn't easily manufacturable in the real world.

⑬ Coupled with this account for manufacturability, true generative design takes into account *simulation* throughout the entire design process. On the front end, that means taking into account your manufacturing method, and the software will take care of simulating a given design's *feasibility*. This only yields designs that meet the necessary simulated criteria and are manufacturable.

Generative Design in the Real World

⑭ Generative design is a new tool at the forefront of engineering tech, but companies are already taking full advantage of what's in front of them. **Notably**, Airbus used generative design to redesign *partitions* in their aircraft. The result was impactful lightweighting that cut 45% of the weight of the part.

⑮ Generative design tools have also been used to design things that traditionally wouldn't be thought of as product design. Architects have used the tool to create the best possible office design new building in Toronto. The algorithms *factored in* employees' wants and needs, and even their preferences on where they work.

⑯ The generative tools laid out 10,000 options for the space and architects sorted through to find the best option. It's the ultimate *melding* of computer-human design.

⑰ Examples of generative design being used in this way are becoming more common, and this tool is being further integrated into our workflows as engineers. The way products are made and engineered is continually being augmented by programs that will shape our future. The future of making things is moving forward at a *blistering* pace.

→ Words and Expressions

realm *n.* a general area of knowledge, activity, or thought（知识、活动、思想的）领域，范围

replicate *vt.* to copy something exactly 复制

onset *n.* the beginning of something 开端，发生

algorithm *n.* a set of instructions that are followed in a fixed order and used for solving a mathematical problem, making a computer program, etc.（尤指计算机）算法，运算法则

inherent *adj.* involved in the constitution or essential character of something, belonging by nature or habit 内在的，固有的

manufacturability *n.* the degree to which a product can be effectively manufactured given its design, cost, and distribution requirements 可制造性

buzzword *n.* a word or phrase from one special area of knowledge that people suddenly think is very important 时髦术语，流行行话

rein *n.* a long narrow band of leather that is fastened around a horse's head in order to control it 缰绳；控制，主宰

augment *vt.* to increase the value, amount, effectiveness, etc. of something 增加，增大，加强

mimic *vt.* to behave or operate in exactly the same way as something or someone else 模拟

interface *vi.* to interact or coordinate harmoniously 相互联系，相互交流

parameter *n.* a set of fixed limits that control the way that something should be done 参数，变量

optimize *vt.* to improve the way that something is done or used so that it is as effective as possible 优化，最佳化

kickstart *vt.* to do something to help a process or activity start or develop more quickly（使）……尽快启动

stark *adj.* unpleasantly clear and impossible to avoid 明显的，鲜明的

simulation *n.* the activity of producing conditions which are similar to real ones, especially in order to test something, or the conditions that are produced 模拟；仿真

feasibility *n.* the state or degree of being easily or conveniently done 可行性

notably *adv.* used to say that a person or thing is a typical example or the most important example of something 尤其，特别地

partition *n.* a thin wall that separates one part of a room from another 隔墙，隔板

factor in 在做决策或评估时，将某个因素纳入考虑范围

meld *vt.* to combine or blend several things in a pleasant or useful way（使）融合；合并

blistering *adj.* extremely fast 极快的

➔ Notes

1. **CAD** (Computer-aided design) 计算机辅助设计
   指运用计算机软件制作并模拟实物设计，展现新开发商品的外型、结构、色彩、质感等特色的过程。

2. **Under Armour** 安德玛
   美国运动用品公司，主要销售运动服、配件及休闲服装，总部位于美国马里兰州。

3. **Airbus** 空中客车
   欧洲民航飞机制造公司，于1970年由法国、德国、西班牙与英国共同创立，总部设于法国图卢兹，是欧洲最大的军火供应制造商空中客车集团旗下企业。

4. **Black & Decker** 百得公司
   全球最大的电动工具制造和销售商，其产品包括配件、五金、家庭装修产品，以及家用电器等，总部位于美国马里兰州巴尔的摩市北部的陶森市，该公司最初成立于1910年。

5. **topology optimization** 拓扑优化
   一种数学方法，可针对一组给定的载荷、边界条件和约束条件优化给定设计空间中的材料布局，以使系统性能最大化。

➔ Reading Skills

Questioning for Critical Reading

Critical reading is an essential skill that involves analyzing and evaluating written material to gain a deeper understanding of the message conveyed. One important aspect of critical reading is questioning, which involves asking thoughtful and insightful questions about the content being read.

Questioning is crucial for critical reading because it helps readers engage with the text and think more deeply about what they are reading. Effective questioning can help clarify confusing or ambiguous ideas, identify the author's purpose or point of view, and evaluate the evidence presented. By asking questions, readers can actively interact with the text and develop a deeper understanding of its meanings and implications.

One approach to questioning is to begin by identifying the main idea or thesis statement of the text. Once this has been established, questions can be asked to probe deeper into the author's argument or to evaluate the evidence presented. For example, the main idea of this article is that generative design has an important effect on engineers, and questions might include:

- What evidence does the author provide to support this claim?

- Are there any alternative perspectives on this issue?

Another approach to questioning is to focus on the language and style used by the author. Questions can be asked to analyze the tone, vocabulary, and sentence structure of the text. For example, the text is a persuasive essay, and questions might include:

- How does the author appeal to the readers' emotions?

- What rhetorical devices are used to make the argument more convincing?

- Is the language used by the author objective or biased?

When questioning a text, it is important to ask open-ended questions that allow for multiple interpretations and perspectives. Closed-ended questions that only require a "yes" or "no" answer are not as effective for critical reading because they do not encourage reflection or analysis. Instead, questions that begin with "how", "why", or "what if" can lead to a more nuanced understanding of the text.

In addition to asking questions, critical reading also involves actively seeking out answers to those questions through research and analysis. This might involve conducting additional research to fill in gaps in knowledge, comparing and contrasting different sources of information, or evaluating credibility and reliability of the author and their sources.

In short, questioning is an essential component of critical reading because readers can make better judgements and gain a deeper understanding of the world around them by developing strong questioning skills.

→ Exercises

I. Building Vocabulary

Choose the best word in the box to fill in each blank. Use each word only once and make proper changes where necessary.

parameter	stark	replicate	notably	optimize
augment	meld	interface	inherent	simulation

1. However, the United States has not been able to _____ that success in other areas, such as diabetes and mental health.

2. This is obviously uncommon, but still illustrates some of the errors _____ in the tool.

3. Cities today are competing for the best talent that can _____ the productivity of their economy.

4. Humans will also continue to _____ with machines to create AI capable of recognizing diverse perspectives.

5. So the next step was to establish the exact behavioral _____ that would indicate that the goats had sensed that Mount Etna was about to erupt.

6. Most of our customers started off wanting to use our products for _____ their production, for reducing their maintenance costs, and for trying to work remotely.

7. Statistics are poor and not easily comparable, but those which do exist show _____ contrasts in conditions between different education authorities.

8. Their projections, based on model _____ of the future, are consistent with changes already being seen in tornado frequency and location.

9. Growth, which rarely continues beyond the age of 20, demands calories and nutrients—_____, protein—to feed expanding tissues.

10. Instead of hearing eight separate opinions, they _____ their ideas into two reports that revealed considerable overlap.

II. Understanding the Text

Read the text again and decide whether the following statements are true (T) or false (F) according to the text.

_____ 1. Generative design is brand new because it replicates an evolutionary approach to design.

_____ 2. It is practical artificial intelligence algorithms that make using mainstream generative design tools possible.

_____ 3. Many companies are willing to adopt generative design as it can offer better ideas, and accomplish their directives better.

_____ 4. Engineers input their criteria, such as material thickness, certain costs, into generative design tools, and then they can get the perfect design.

_____ 5. Building a chair is a basic example of practical implementation of generative design.

_____ 6. Like topology optimization, latticing, or other similar CAD tools, generative design creates a new design.

_____ 7. Both manufacturability and simulation are considered in generative design throughout the entire design process.

III. Theme Exploration

While generative design offers many advantages, as the author states, there are also some potential disadvantages to consider. For example, it relies heavily on technology, including algorithms and software, and is therefore vulnerable to technical issues, such as software bugs or compatibility problems. Work in groups and discuss any other disadvantages you can think of.

IV. Real-Life Project

In the author's opinion, generative design seems to be better than any other CAD tool in the field of design. Is this true? Do you agree or disagree? Think critically and do further research on generative design and other CAD tools. Then choose one of the other CAD tools and compare it with generative design. Report your findings to the class.

Part II
Writing

Introduction

1. Functions of the Introduction Section

The introduction is written to capture readers' attention and prepare them for the rest of the paper. This section has three main goals: introducing the research topic, summarizing what is known about the research topic, and previewing how further research on the topic can be conducted. More specifically, an effective introduction can create the research context for understanding the entire paper by providing readers with the necessary background knowledge, building connections between the present research and prior research, stating the purpose and rationale of the present research, specifying research questions, and indicating possible research outcomes. Therefore, the introduction section is regarded as the foundation of the entire paper.

2. Structure of the Introduction Section

The Creating a Research Space (CARS) model is a rhetorical pattern found to be very common in the introductions of academic research papers (Swales, 1990; Swales &

Feak, 2012). It was identified through extensive studies of published research papers across different disciplines. According to Swales & Feak, research paper introductions usually follow a three-move structure, with each move being realized by one or several steps. These steps are either obligatory (often required) or optional (probable in some fields, but rare in others):

Moves	Steps
Move 1: establishing a research territory	a. By showing that the general research area is important, central, interesting, problematic, or relevant in some way (**optional**); b. By introducing and reviewing items of previous research in the area (**obligatory**).
Move 2: establishing a niche	By indicating a gap in previous research or by extending previous knowledge in some way (**obligatory**).
Move 3: occupying the niche	a. By outlining the purpose or nature of the present research (**obligatory**); b. By listing research questions or hypothesis (**optional**); c. By announcing principal findings (**optional**); d. By stating the value of the present research (**optional**); e. By indicating the structure of the research paper (**optional**).

In terms of organization, the introduction of a research paper is like a funnel in which information flows from the general to the specific. It moves from general background information, including an introduction to the field of research and a brief review of the most relevant and representative literature, towards the specific research problems or gaps, then towards the very specific objectives, significance, and/or research questions of the present study. It should be noted that Swale's three-move structure is just a general framework, and the actual steps that an introduction includes will vary slightly depending on the field of discipline, so novice writers should apply it flexibly in their own introduction writing. Look at the structural components in the following example:

[❶-❸ *Broad background information*] ❶Plastic waste is one of the primary sources of pollution and biodiversity loss. Cleaning rivers, oceans, and cities of plastic waste has been attempted by many countries with varying degrees of success. ❷The plastic waste, if sorted and graded, can be used to produce value-added products; this process has created opportunities for small and medium-sized enterprises (SMEs) to develop innovative business models.

❸Developing a circular economy (CE) around plastic is the key challenge for firms around the world (WEF, 2016).

【❹-❺ *Specific background information*】❹Digitalization is opening up new opportunities for SMEs to innovate and flourish (OECD, 2019, p. 7). ❺Therefore, SMEs are adopting different emerging technologies, including 3D printing and blockchain, to support their engagement in CE-related initiatives. 【❻-❼ *Importance and significance of the research field*】❻The natural environmental orientation of firms leads to higher profitability in the long term (Menguc & Ozanne, 2005). ❼Indeed, digital and environmental orientation has a positive direct effect on product innovation performance. 【❽*Problem in the research field*】❽However, pursuing a dual strategy towards digitalization and environmental sustainability was not found to be significant for product innovation performance (Ardito et al., 2021). 【❾-⓮ *Review of the relevant previous research*】❾Ranta et al. (2018) studied the business models of CE-driven business ventures in terms of their value proposition, value creation and delivery, and value capture; they do not explicitly consider the value such models provide to customers, and nor do they consider the role of digital technologies in enhancing the value of CE initiatives. ❿Therefore, it is unclear how SMEs can generate value for customers from a CE-oriented business model by utilizing digital technologies and what kind of capabilities they need to develop to generate such a competitive advantage.

⓫Recent studies have shown the positive influence of digital technologies in the circular economy sector. ⓬Nandi et al. (2020) proposed a resource-based framework for blockchain implementation in supply chains. ⓭Kristoffersen et al. (2020) developed a digital-enabled circular strategies framework for manufacturing companies and considered the Internet of Things (IoT), big data, and data analytics, while Bag, Pretorius, et al. (2021) analyzed the role of big-data analytics-powered artificial intelligence for sustainable manufacturing and CE adoption in manufacturing companies. ⓮Indeed, there is a small but growing number of entrepreneurs who are working within the 3D printing (3DP) ecosystem to create a CE (Despeisse et al., 2017) and using blockchain to facilitate its implementation (Kouhizadeh et al., 2020).

【⓯-⓰ *Research gap*】⓯However, the resources and capabilities needed to adopt 3DP and blockchain for the circular economy is not known. ⓰Kouhizadeh et al. (2020) also concluded that a more critical examination of blockchain's potential in a CE context is needed.

【⓱*Purpose of the present research*】⓱In this research, therefore, we explore the capabilities needed by SMEs to implement 3DP and blockchain to generate competitive advantage from their CE-based business models. 【⓲-⓴ *Research questions*】⓲The specific research questions we consider are as follows: ⓳ a) Which capabilities are needed by SMEs implementing a circular economy to adopt digital technologies such as blockchain and 3D printing? ⓴b) How do the circular economy and digital technology-based resources and capabilities of SMEs provide value to their customers?

【㉑ *Approaches to the present research*】㉑We conducted in-depth interviews with SMEs involved in recycling plastic waste and utilizing 3DP and blockchain, and we drew insights from

> those cases using qualitative analysis and so develop testable propositions. [㉒*Major findings of the present research*] ㉒The results show that, combined with digital resources and explorative capabilities, CE resources and exploitative capabilities help SMEs create value. [㉓ *Contribution of the present research*] ㉓Furthermore, we extend the resource-based view (RBV) by using organizational ambidexterity to explain how CE and digital technology adoption by SMEs can provide value to customers.

3. Verb Tenses in the Introduction Section

The introduction of a research paper may contain a mixture of several verb tenses, each providing a different context for the statements it accompanies. Here are some general guidelines for the tense usage:

Moves	Functions	Tenses
Introducing background information	Introducing a research topic or stating the fact(s) widely accepted in a research field	Simple present tense / Present perfect tense
	Defining technical terms related to a research topic	Simple present tense
	Describing general research significance	Simple present tense / Present perfect tense
Reviewing previous research	Reporting what previous researchers did, investigated, studied, analyzed, etc.	Simple past tense
	Making general statements, conclusions, or interpretations about findings of previous research	Simple present tense / Present perfect tense
Indicating a gap	Indicating that something is missing or unclear in the previous research or extending the existing research	Simple present tense / Present perfect tense
Introducing the present research	Indicating the focus, main argument, or purpose of the present research	Simple present tense
	Listing research questions, or hypothesis of the present research	Simple present tense
	Stating the importance of current research and its contribution to the research field	Simple present tense
	Indicating the structure of the present paper	Simple present tense

→ Exercises

I. Read the introduction section from an academic paper titled "The Development of the Chinese Copula shì Construction: A Diachronic Constructional Perspective" and discuss the following questions.

> In recent years there has been growing interest in construction grammar, a branch of cognitive linguistics. It is a model of the speaker's knowledge of language, and its architecture is based in form-meaning pairings or signs in the extended sense of words, phrases, clauses, and complex sentences (see e.g. Croft 2001; Fillmore et al. 1988; Fillmore & Kay 1997; Goldberg 1995, 2006; Sag 2012). It has begun to be adopted in analyses of Chinese (see e.g. Chen 2009; Lu 2004; especially Zhan & Sun 2013 on the copula shì in cleft constructions). Although most work on construction grammar to date has been synchronic, there is a growing body of research from a diachronic perspective. The study of the development of constructions has been undertaken mainly in connection with European and European-derived languages (see e.g. Barðdal 2008; Barðdal et al. 2015; Bergs & Diewald 2008; Hilpert 2013; Petré 2014; Traugott & Trousdale 2013). Constructional historical studies of Chinese include Bisang (2010), Peng (2013) and Zhan & Traugott (2015) on how the Chinese cleft construction developed over time. The present study focuses on the development of the copula shì construction prior to the development of the cleft. It is a contribution to constructional studies in Chinese, and explores ways in which the perspective of work on constructionalization differs from the perspective of work on grammaticalization.
>
> The paper is structured as follows. Section 2 outlines some basic points about the perspectives on grammar and change adopted. Section 3 provides a brief overview of the data sources and methodology. Section 4 provides a detailed analysis of the development of the copula shì construction. Section 5 presents a quantitative analysis of this development. Section 6 is the conclusion.

1. What moves and steps are included in the introduction?

2. What signal words or expressions are used to introduce each step of the introduction?

3. What verb tenses are used in the introduction?

II. Find some published research papers in your field of research and analyze the introduction section of each paper based on the following questions. Present your findings to the class.

1. What structural moves and steps are presented in the introduction? In what order are they presented? Which step(s) is obligatory or optional in the introduction of research papers in your research field?

2. What is the organizational pattern of the introduction?

3. Are there any signal words or expressions used to indicate the beginning of each step?

4. What verb tenses are used in the introduction?

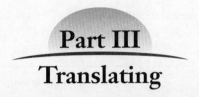

Part III Translating

学术论文引言翻译

引言是学术论文正文的第一部分。英汉学术论文引言在结构上具有一定的共性，两者都包含研究背景、评述前期文献、说明前期研究中存在的问题或局限、介绍研究目的等内容。本节主要结合实例，通过对比呈现汉语学术论文引言常见语步中一些句子的翻译。

1. 与研究背景相关的句子常涉及基本概念介绍、研究主题和研究问题的引入等内容，因此在翻译时时态上一般选用一般现在时或现在完成时。常见句型如下：

- X is / has become a key/central issue in...

- Recently / In recent years, there has been growing interest in...

- There has been extensive research on...

- The past decade has seen the rapid development of X in...

请看下面的例子：

近年来，智慧交通系统领域的技术发展和研究活动主要集中在机动交通方面。	In recent years, both technological development and research activities in the field of Intelligent Transport Systems (ITS) have primarily focused on motorized transport.
近年来，矿物能源枯竭和环境污染等问题越来越突出，提高能源使用效率和开发可再生能源成为人类面临的重要课题。	In recent years, the problems of mineral resource depletion and environmental pollution have become increasingly prominent. Improving energy efficiency and developing renewable energy have emerged as key issues facing mankind.

2. 在介绍前期相关研究时，英语学术论文多用一般过去时或现在完成时，因此在翻译汉语中类似句子时可根据上下文灵活运用一些功能句型，常见的如：

- X reported/highlighted/showed/suggested/demonstrated/explored/conducted/argued/proposed/investigated/…

- The research to date has been conducted using…

- Recent research has focused on…

请看下面的例子：

国内外学者针对电力系统灵活性开展了一系列研究。李海波（2015）等从可靠性和统计学的角度提出一种电力系统灵活性定量评估指标体系。	Scholars at home and abroad have conducted a series of studies on power system flexibility. Li Haibo et al. (2015) proposed a quantitative evaluation index system for power system flexibility from the perspective of reliability and statistics.
前期对该主题的研究有限，且主要集中在性别偏见影响学生进步的具体机制上。	Prior research on this topic is limited, and it has focused on specific mechanisms through which gender bias could affect students' progress.

3. 英译有关前期研究中的不足或存在的问题时，时态上用一般现在时或现在完成时，常采用含有否定意味的词或词组，如 limitation、inadequacy、lack、neglect、little、unable、unsatisfactory、problematic、controversial、however、suffer from、fail to，以及常用的句式，如：

- Prior/previous studies have failed to…

- … however, very little research has been conducted on…

- X has not yet been empirically studied/examined…

请看下面的例子：

然而这些研究都未注意主播的言语行为。尽管 Guo（2022）等人关注过主播的言语，但他们只是选取幽默和激情话语来研究主播的交际风格，没有把言语视为一种行为，或考察言语行为。	However, none of these studies have paid attention to the speech acts of streamers. Although Guo et al. (2022) have considered streamer speech, they have only extracted humor and passion as streamer communication styles and have not treated speech as a behavior or examined speech acts.

上述研究多集中于灵活性概念的阐释和评价方法的改善，而在电力系统规划、运行等场景的使用方面涉及较少。	Most of the aforementioned studies have focused on interpreting the concept of flexibility and improving evaluation methods. Little research has been conducted on their applications in scenarios such as power system planning and operation.

4. 汉语论文引言在介绍研究目的时，常采用"本文/本研究旨在……""本研究关注/尝试/主要针对……"等表达方式。翻译研究目的和研究重点的句子时多采用一般现在时，可参考下列表示目的的名词或动词，如：

- The purpose/objective/aim of the study is to...

- This study attempts/seeks/intends/aims to...

- This paper explores/discusses/addresses/presents/proposes...

请看下面的例子：

本文讨论了用于支持智能制造的关键技术，如物联网（IoT）、信息物理系统、云计算、大数据分析（BDA）和信息通信技术（ICT）。	This paper discusses key technologies used to support intelligent manufacturing, including the Internet of Things (IoT), cyber-physical systems, cloud computing, big data analytics (BDA), and information and communications technology (ICT).
本研究以一个典型废弃冶炼场所为研究对象，通过为土壤-地下水系统建立一个三维可变饱和溶质运移数值模型，来有效预测污染风险趋势。	This study focuses on a typical abandoned smelting site and aims to effectively predict the pollution risk trends by developing a three-dimensional, variable saturated solute transport numerical model for the soil-groundwater system.

5. 英语中在介绍论文主要结构时常用一般现在时，可使用主动语态，直接以"section X"或"part X"为主语，如"Section X examines/summarizes/describes/reviews/explains/shows/presents…"；有时为了丰富句式，也可选用被动语态，将某部分的主要内容放在主语位置。

请看下面的例子：

论文的其余部分结构如下：第2部分对可撤销指纹模板生成进行了文献综述。第3部分介绍了所提出的在特征级使用融合结构的方法。第4部分为实验评估和分析……	The rest of this paper is structured as follows: Section 2 provides a literature survey on the generation of cancelable fingerprint templates. The proposed method of using fused structures at the feature level is demonstrated in Section 3. The experimental evaluation and analysis are presented in Section 4…
本文分为六个部分：第2部分是文献综述。第3部分介绍研究方法，包括研究数据及数据分析框架。第4部分进行数据分析。第5部分是讨论。最后第6部分陈述结论。	The paper falls into 6 sections. A review of the literature is provided in Section 2. Section 3 presents research methods, including research data and the framework of data analysis. Section 4 is data analysis. Section 5 addresses discussion. Finally, a conclusion is presented in Section 6.

→ Exercises

Analyze the functions of the following sentences and translate them into English.

1. 尽管基于机器学习的预测模型在医学领域中使用得越来越多，但是临床医生仍然觉得很难依赖这些模型。

2. 最新研究强调了供应链（supply chain）在应对全球化和动态运营环境所带来的不可预测事件时所面临的挑战。

3. 本研究尝试建立一个坚实的理论背景来区分这些概念，并阐明它们是如何结合在一起的。

4. 本研究为解决供应链管理（supply chain management）领域的可持续性和弹性问题的学者和从业者提供了思路。

5. 论文的其余部分结构如下：第二部分概述了可解释性机器学习（interpretable machine learning）方面的相关文献以及其在医疗保健领域中的应用；第三部分对提出的可解释性深度学习框架进行了详细描述。

Unit 6
On-Demand Economy

Part I
Reading

Eight Service Industries That Drive the On-Demand Economy

Manish Vyas

① The **on-demand** services industry has overtaken traditional business models by providing goods and services to people at their convenience. Not just 1 or 2 but numerous industries have shaped from physical to digital in order to meet the evolving needs of the market.

② From ride-**hailing** to food delivery, and transportation to booking doctors' appointments, one can **avail** all these services on-demand at their fingertips. It can be said, the future is all digital and on-demand. As per the recent survey, 51% of entrepreneurs who offer on-demand services have experienced their financial situation improved far better than the previous year.

③ Moreover, the market for on-demand services is expected to reach a **whopping** $335 billion by 2025, according to the PwC report. Now without any more **addons**, let us jump to the service industries that are driving the on-demand economy.

Healthcare

④ In the healthcare industry, the on-demand economy has **manifested** in a number of ways. For example, **telemedicine** services allow patients to consult with healthcare providers remotely, often through video conferencing or phone calls. This makes it easier for patients to access healthcare services without having to physically visit a healthcare facility. Another way that the healthcare industry has contributed to the growth of the on-demand economy is through the use of online pharmacies and home delivery services. These services allow patients to order prescription medications online and have them delivered to their homes, making it easier and more convenient for them to access the medications they need.

⑤ In 2022, it was estimated that the revenue will reach 52.65 billion dollars and it is expected to reach 94.07 billion by 2027 at an annual growth rate (CAGR 2022–2027) of 12.31%—as per Statista.

Hyperlocal Industry

⑥ The *hyperlocal* industry, which refers to businesses and services that operate within a specific geographic area, has played a significant role in the growth of the on-demand economy. These businesses and services are able to offer highly targeted and personalized services to customers by leveraging their local knowledge and resources.

⑦ According to recent statistics, the global hyperlocal delivery apps market revenue totaled $952.7 million in 2021 and is expected to reach $8856.6 million by 2023 at a growing CAGR of 22.6% over the forecast period (2022–2032).

⑧ This growth is driven by a variety of factors, including the increasing use of mobile devices and the *proliferation* of on-demand app platforms, as well as the growing demand for convenience and speed among consumers.

eCommerce Industry

⑨ The eCommerce industry has been a driving force behind the emergence and popularity of the on-demand economy, in which consumers can easily order goods and services online and receive them quickly.

⑩ In recent years, eCommerce sales have seen significant growth, with online sales globally reaching 5.2 trillion U.S. dollars in 2021 and is estimated to reach 8.1 trillion dollars by 2026.

⑪ The strange part is that eCommerce had no existence before the birth of on-demand services. Experts say that the success of on-demand and eCommerce goes hand in hand.

⑫ With time, eCommerce has also evolved as the entire on-demand industry is evolving. This often change in the customer's demand has forced experts to work on eCommerce mobile app trends. If you ever have a plan to start an eCommerce business or build an eCommerce app, you should first check the trends and then take the next step.

Education Industry

⑬ In recent years, the demand for online education services has increased significantly due to the convenience and flexibility they offer. With e-learning, students can access educational content and courses from anywhere and at any time, making it easier for them to fit learning into their busy schedules.

⑭ E-learning services have also benefited from the growth of the on-demand economy in other ways. For example, the rise of on-demand video streaming platforms like Netflix and Hulu has made it easier for e-learning providers to deliver video-based content to their students.

⑮ In addition, the proliferation of mobile devices and high-speed Internet access has made it easier for students to access e-learning content and courses **on the go**.

Fitness Services

⑯ Finding time for fitness can be a challenge for many people, which is why on-demand fitness services have become so popular. These services allow people to access **workouts** and fitness content from the comfort of their own homes, rather than having to go to a **brick-and-mortar** gym or studio. Fitness apps, in-fitness streaming platforms, and other technologies make it easy for people to get the workouts they need on their own schedule, without paying a large fee or committing to a strict schedule. People can choose from a wide range of qualified trainers, rather than being limited to those who are local.

Transportation

⑰ Transportation services have led to a significant increase in the demand for the on-demand economy, and have also created new earning opportunities for drivers. In recent years, the demand for on-demand transportation services such as ride-hailing and car-sharing has exploded, fueled by the convenience and accessibility of these services through smartphone apps.

⑱ According to a report by Statista, the ride-hailing and taxi segment **revenue** have recorded $276.40 billion in 2022. Furthermore, the revenue is expected to reach $378.80 billion by 2027 at an annual growth rate (CAGR 2022–2027) of 6.51%.

⑲ As per the study made by Grand View Research, the on-demand transportation market size is expected to grow at a CAGR of 19.8% from 2018 to 2025.

Travel Industry

⑳   The travel service industry has embraced the on-demand economy by offering a variety of services that can be easily booked and managed through mobile apps and websites.

㉑   According to a report by Statista, the travel market is expected to be worth $854.8 billion in 2023, with most of that money coming from hotel bookings. The report also says that the market will be worth more than $1,016 billion by 2027, with online bookings accounting for the majority of that revenue.

Logistics

㉒   The on-demand economy has significantly transformed the *courier* and *logistics* industry by making it more efficient and smooth. Technology has played a key role in this transformation, enabling small players to enter the market and providing live customer notifications and SMS tracking.

㉓   Prior to the rise of the on-demand economy, delivery times and booking processes were major concerns for customers, as were the confusing and often *disparate* pricing structures within the industry. However, with the *advent* of on-demand services, these issues have been largely resolved.

㉔   Companies can now easily book a truck at any time to transport their *cargo*, and they can track the package from the moment it is *dispatched* until it reaches its destination. Deliv, Postmates, GetWagon, and TruckBuddy have already achieved success in the logistics industry by developing an on-demand delivery app.

Final Words

㉕   As we have seen, the on-demand services industry is an *integral* part of modern life and touches almost every aspect of our daily routines. With the emergence of new technologies like AI and IoT, the way we interact with the world is changing rapidly, and this is reflected in the evolution of the on-demand services industry.

→ Words and Expressions

on-demand *adj.* done or happening whenever sb. asks 按需的

hail *vt.* to signal to a taxi or a bus, in order to get the driver to stop 招手（请出租车或公共汽车停下）

avail *vt.* to use or take advantage of (an opportunity or available resource) 利用

whopping *adj.* [only before noun] very large 巨大的

addon *n.* a piece of equipment that you connect to a computer to improve its performance 附加组件，插件

manifest *vt.* to show something clearly, through signs or actions 显示，表现

telemedicine *n.* the use of communications technology, especially the telephone and Internet, to provide healthcare（通过电信手段对病人诊断、治疗的）远程医疗，远距离治病

hyperlocal *adj.* characteristic of or associated with a small area within a particular locality 超本地化的；集中在特定小区域的

proliferation *n.* a sudden increase in the amount or number of something（数量的）激增，剧增

on the go while going from place to place; while traveling 在行动中

workout *n.* a period of physical exercise, especially as training for a sport 锻炼，训练

brick-and-mortar *adj.* describing the physical presence of a building or other structures（有）实体的

revenue *n.* money that a business or organization receives over a period of time, especially from selling goods or services（企业、组织的）收入，收益

courier *n.* a person or company that is paid to take packages somewhere 快递公司；快递员

logistics *n.* the business of transporting things such as goods to the place where they are needed 物流

disparate *adj.* consisting of things or people that are very different and not related to each other 迥然不同的

advent *n.* a coming or arrival 出现，到来

cargo *n.* the goods that are being carried in a ship or plane（船或飞机装载的）货物

dispatch *vt.* to send someone or something somewhere for a particular purpose 发送；派遣

integral *adj.* forming a necessary part of something 必需的，必要的

→ Notes

1. **PwC** (Pricewaterhouse Coopers) 普华永道
   国际会计审计专业服务网络，四大国际会计师事务所之一，其他三大事务所是毕马威、德勤和安永。

2. **CAGR** (compound annual growth rate) 复合年均增长率
   指一项投资在特定时期内的年度增长率，用来比较和评估某一板块或某一市场指数下的不同股票之间的相对表现。进行产业分析时，此指标可以消除国家与产业的差异，客观评估投资效益，是广为使用的分析报告指标。

3. **Netflix** 网飞公司
   美国奈飞公司，简称网飞，创立于1997年，是一家以创始人名字命名的会员订阅制流媒体播放平台、在线视频播放服务商，总部位于美国加利福尼亚州洛斯盖图。

4. **Hulu** 葫芦网
   起源于美国，是由NBC（National Broadcasting Company）环球和新闻集团以及迪士尼联合投资的一家网络视频网站。它和全美许多著名电视台及电影公司达成协议，通过授权点播模式向用户提供视频资源。

5. **Statista**
   一家总部位于德国的在线数据平台，主要提供统计数据、市场研究和商业情报，帮助企业、学术机构和政府部门进行数据驱动的决策。

6. **SMS** (Short Messaging Service) 短讯服务
   有时也称为信息、短信、短消息、文字消息，该服务也有许多英语的俗称，如SMSes、text messages、messages、texts 和 txts，是移动电话服务的一种。短信服务最早是在GSM手机系统上引入的，现在几乎在任何手机系统上都能通用。

7. **Deliv**
   成立于2012年，是一家总部位于美国加州门洛帕克市的众包快递公司，为百思买（Best Buy）、梅西百货（Macy's）、家得宝（Home Depot）等多家知名企业提供快递服务。

8. **Postmates**
   一家美国外卖服务公司，成立于2011年，于2020年被Uber收购。它提供餐厅食物配送和其他商品的本地送货服务。

9. **IoT** (Internet of Things) 物联网

   通过信息传感设备，按约定的协议，将任何物体与网络相连接，物体通过信息传播媒介进行信息交换和通信，以实现智能化识别、定位、跟踪、监管等功能。物联网将现实世界数字化，其应用范围十分广泛，如运输和物流、工业制造、健康医疗、智能环境、个人和社会领域等。

→ **Reading Skills**

Distinguishing Facts from Opinions

Nowadays, with the abundance of information at our fingertips, it is easy to become overwhelmed and confused about what is true and what is not. However, it is important to be able to differentiate between two types of statements, "fact" and "opinion", in order to make informed decisions and have productive discussions, especially when we are reading.

Firstly, let us define what we mean by "fact" and "opinion". A fact is a statement that can be proven or demonstrated to be true. For example, "the Earth is round" is a fact that can be verified by scientific evidence. An opinion, on the other hand, is a personal belief or feeling about something. For example, "Pizza is the best food" is an opinion, as it cannot be proven to be objectively true or false.

One way to distinguish between fact and opinion is to look for evidence. Facts are supported by evidence, such as data, research, or observations. For instance, in Para. 3 of the text, the author shows us the growing trend of the market for on-demand services with data from the PwC report. By contrast, opinions are not necessarily supported by evidence and may vary depending on individual perspectives and experiences. In Para. 6, the author believes that the hyperlocal industry has played a significant role in the growth of the on-demand economy, which is an instance of his personal opinion.

Another technique is to consider the language used in a statement. Statements that use objective, neutral language are more likely to be facts. For example, in Para. 9, "In recent years, eCommerce sales have seen significant growth" is an objective statement that can be backed up with the evidence of "online sales globally reaching 5.2 trillion U.S. dollars in 2021". In contrast, statements that use subjective language, such as "finding time for fitness can be a challenge for many people" in Para. 16, are more likely to be opinions.

It's also important to consider the source of the information. Is it from a reliable or credible source? Is the source timely or out of date? Can the claims be backed up with evidence? If the information is from those who have a vested interest in certain aspects, such as a company promoting its own product, their statements may be biased and less trustworthy.

In conclusion, distinguishing between fact and opinion is a critical reading skill. By looking for evidence and considering language and sources, we can have a more objective and accurate understanding of the text.

→ Exercises

I. Building Vocabulary

Choose the best word in the box to fill in each blank. Use each word only once and make proper changes where necessary.

| disparate | advent | cargo | dispatch | avail |
| manifest | proliferation | access | segment | integral |

1. Drafting cables to be _____ to Washington is one of the principal occupations of the foreign service officer in the field.

2. The problem is not demand: The need for special effects has gone through the roof and become _____ to the film industry.

3. Mountain sickness is usually _____ as headache, tiredness, and loss of appetite.

4. Furthermore, the differences become even more _____ as the complexity of the vocabulary and sentences increase.

5. The _____ of scientific thinking has institutionalized the idea that knowledge has to progress and can do so only through research.

6. Steel was stronger so boats could be built with thinner plates, making them lighter and so able to carry more _____.

7. Residents visiting the library could _____ themselves of the park district's facilities and programs.

8. Shortening product life cycles and rapid product _____ mean that investment in innovation is critical in global competition.

9. Microprocessor sales represent one of the largest _____ of the chip market.

10. Businesses and consumers say the smartphone has become the primary device they use to _____ the Internet.

II. Understanding the Text

Read the following sentences from the text and determine which of them are facts.

1. The on-demand services industry has overtaken traditional business models by providing goods and services to people at their convenience. (Para. 1)

2. It can be said, the future is all digital and on-demand. (Para. 2)

3. … the market for on-demand services is expected to reach a whopping $335 billion by 2025, according to the PwC report. (Para. 3)

4. In 2022, it was estimated that the revenue will reach 52.65 billion dollars and it is expected to reach 94.07 billion by 2027 at an annual growth rate (CAGR 2022–2027) of 12.31%—as per Statista. (Para. 5)

5. The eCommerce industry has been a driving force behind the emergence and popularity of the on-demand economy, … (Para. 9)

6. Finding time for fitness can be a challenge for many people, which is why on-demand fitness services have become so popular. (Para. 16)

7. … the demand for on-demand transportation services such as ride-hailing and car-sharing has exploded, … (Para. 17)

III. Theme Exploration

There is no denying that the on-demand economy, driven by new developments in finance and technology, has to some extent brought convenience to people. Meanwhile, it also represents a growing regulatory challenge. Work in groups and discuss what is particularly troubling about the on-demand economy and what can be done in terms of regulatory policy for its development.

IV. Real-Life Project

The author of the text describes the status quo of the on-demand economy and eight service industries that drive the on-demand economy in his country from his point of view. Now it's your turn to do some research on the development of the on-demand economy in China. Please search for relevant information and prepare a three-minute presentation about your research results.

Part II
Writing

Literature Review

1. Functions of Literature Review

A literature review is the critical review of previously published works related to a particular topic or subject area within a certain time period. The "Literature" in a literature review may cover journal papers, books, theses, dissertations, or conference proceedings. The literature review of research papers is often included in the introduction section, while in some research papers, it may appear after the introduction section as a separate part with a heading such as "Literature Review", "Related Research" or "Related Work". A literature review basically fulfils the following three major functions:

First, it highlights what has been studied and what knowledge or ideas have been established on a particular research topic, providing the foundation for the present research. Second, it indicates the gaps (undiscovered or under-researched areas), disputes, and open questions left from previous studies based on the evaluation of the existing literature, justifying the significance and necessity of the present research. Third, it places the present research within the larger context of relevant literature, enabling the writer's own ideas or research findings to be integrated into the existing body of knowledge.

2. Structure of Literature Review

The literature review of research papers generally follows a basic introduction-body-conclusion structure. The introduction states the topic or scope of the literature review, thus providing a context for reviewing the literature. As the focus of the literature review, the body part is much more than a list and summary of individual sources. It also entails synthesizing various sources by categorizing them around a specific theme or point of contention and critically evaluating the strengths and weaknesses of the sources. The conclusion summarizes the key findings from the literature or concludes the overall state of the literature, and states what gaps the current research will address. Due to the limit on the length of research papers, the introduction and conclusion may be very short, including just a few sentences. The following text is an excerpt of a literature review extracted from the introduction of a research paper.

> [❶-❹ *Introducing the research topic*] ❶To cover grey energy issues, life cycle analysis (LCA) is an acknowledged method that is based on international standards (ISO 14040, ISO 14044). ❷It includes the assessment of total energy consumption during the whole life cycle of a product (Piccardo and Gustavsson, 2021). ❸The manufacturing phase is part of this. ❹However, how and in which life cycle phases e.g. grey energy is accounted for is open to broad interpretation (Achenbach et al., 2016). [❺-❻ *Summarizing and synthesizing the relevant literature*] ❺Methods derived from this, such as life cycle energy assessment (LCEA) and life cycle carbon emissions assessment (LCCO2A), are specifications with focus on the corresponding aspects (Chau et al., 2015; Cabeza et al., 2014; Florentin et al., 2017). ❻Using the LCA method, Environmental Product Declarations (EPDs) are defined according to DIN EN 15804: 2014–07.
> [❼-❾ *Evaluating the relevant literature*] ❼The advantage of these methods and data is the clearly defined and recognized principles they are based on. ❽However, they focus on primary material-based products first... ❾First studies are available that calculate the energy input

Unit 6　On-Demand Economy

> and resulting emissions of the RC process based on LCA, but with focus only on the waste management process (Wang et al., 2022). [❿-⓬ *Concluding the review and introducing the current research*] ❿So far, there is no research available on the indirect effects of the use of RC materials on building product manufacture and the resulting impacts on the grey energy performance of the end product in the specific implementation context. ⓫Against the backdrop of global warming and the need to implement every stricter climate protection regulation, the issue of grey energy is becoming ever more prominent (IRP, 2020; Acharya et al., 2018). ⓬This is the issue to be tackled in the current paper...

Be aware of some pitfalls when writing a literature review. First, avoid simply listing each piece of literature. Second, avoid citing irrelevant and trivial sources. Instead of covering every paper and book written on the research topic, a literature review should comprise the most important and relevant sources. Third, avoid direct copying from the source texts. When citing other writers' research work, summarizing and paraphrasing are preferred over direct quoting.

3. Organization of Literature Review

Thematic approach, methodological approach, and chronological approach are the three approaches widely adopted to organize the body of a literature review. Which approach to use depends on what the writer aims to accomplish with the review. Besides, a combined use of these approaches can be found in some literature reviews.

1) Thematic Approach

A thematic approach groups the literature according to conceptual categories and themes. It is the most common way to organize the literature review. In this approach, one paragraph or one subsection usually deals with one aspect of the research topic. For example:

> ... The packaging opening process has been addressed by many studies. Many of these show that older adults experience difficulties and limitations in the packaging interaction (Berns, 1981; Voorbij and Steenbekkers, 2002; Fair et al., 2008; Carse et al., 2011). Although the packaging design... Other studies have also evaluated the torque transmission by the hands and fingers (Su et al., 2009), as well as the relationship between the materials and the opening process (Andreasson and Jönsson, 2014).
>
> In the case of CRPs, many studies have shown concern about the usability of this kind of packaging, highlighting the danger that children still can access the content of such products (Assargaard and Sjoberg, 1995; Rodgers, 1996; Schmidt et al., 2004)...

2) Methodological Approach

Literature reviews that are organized methodologically focus on the methods used in the existing literature. Writers may compare the methods and evaluate their efficiency. This approach works best when new methods are used on a research question that has already been explored. For example:

> ... Currently, many kinds of microfabrication approaches have been employed to pattern cell arrays, including microfluidic technique (Wang et al., 2022), photolithography (Raittinen et al., 2021), inject printing (Sun et al., 2018) and microcontact printing (μCP) (Yang et al., 2016). Among these methods, microfluidic technique requires highly integrated multidisciplinary technologies and high cost (Berlanda et al., 2021), while photolithography demands sophisticated procedures (Larramendy et al., 2015). In contrast, μCP approaches provide much easier access for the construction of cell array chip devices...

3) Chronological Approach

A chronological approach is used to highlight how research in a certain field has evolved over time. Instead of simply summarizing each related work in time sequence, this approach often aims to find out the important patterns, key debates, or turning points that have shaped the research direction of the field at specific periods. For example:

> ... The historical study of animal cognition has received increasing attention in recent years (Richards, 1987; Ingensiep, 1996; Cheung, 2006; Riskin, 2016; Buchenau & Lo Presti, 2017; Van den Berg, 2018, 2020). However, historical studies of animal language are rare. Exceptions include the study of animal language from Darwin to the present in Radick, 2007, the discussion of animal language and the collapse of the animal-human boundary in the early-modern period by Wolfe, 2017, with a focus on the French and English context, and the discussion of bird song from Aristotle to Kant in Smith, 2017. In contrast to these authors, I adopt a history of ideas approach and discuss how the study of animal communication became a subject related to the investigation of animals and the origin and development of language...

→ Exercises

I. The following excerpt is taken from the literature review of an academic paper titled "Short-Term Anchor Linking and Long-Term Self-Guided Attention for Video Object Detection". Read it carefully and discuss the questions.

> The main idea behind most of the state-of-the-art spatio-temporal object detection frameworks is to include feature aggregation throughout several input frames to enhance the per-frame features. Some works such as [34] and [40] use optical flow information to find correspondences between... Recent methods try to avoid the optical flow calculation time, ... Alternatively, [36] proposes a Recurrent Neural Network (RNN), defining a module... A more recent work [13] proposes a new module, ... All these methods aim to find correspondences and aggregate features at pixel level.
>
> Several approaches have proposed to work at object level instead of pixel level [18], [17], [31], [8], [29], [4], [5], linking objects throughout time. Object level methods aggregate only useful information in areas with ... We follow this object-oriented approach in our architecture.
>
> Object tracking techniques have been applied to link detections calculated at frame level in [17], [18]. As an alternative to object tracking, a Tubelet Proposal Network (TPN) was first introduced in [16]... It takes advantage of the generally large receptive field of CNNs and the spatio-temporal redundancy between consecutive frames to be able to handle moving objects using static proposals throughout neighboring frames. A similar idea is present in [31] ... In our implementation, we avoid tubelet proposals, working directly with box proposals. This reduces...
>
> Previous work only considers short- or long-term information to implement attention mechanisms, but not the combination of both to take full advantage of the whole spatio-temporal context. This issue is tackled in [4] by integrating... Nevertheless, ..., they just get rid of geometric features, proposing a location free implementation. As a step forward, we propose a new method to integrate these geometric features in the long-term aggregation method. Our approach updates bounding box positions throughout time, making possible to use previous locations to establish proposal relationships.

1. How does the author organize the literature review?

2. What are the functions of the underlined sentences?

3. What verb tenses are used in the literature review? List the tenses used in each part of the literature review.

II. Find some published journal papers in your field of research and analyze the literature review of each paper based on the following questions. Present your findings to the class.

1. Where is the literature review placed in each paper? Is it a separate section or included in the introduction section?

2. What are the basic structural moves in the literature review? What signals or contextual clues helped you identify them?

3. What approach is adopted to organize the literature review? Which approach has a higher frequency of occurrence?

4. What verb tenses are used in the literature review?

Part III
Translating

被动句和定语从句翻译

一、被动句的翻译

被动语态在英语学术论文中的使用频率非常高,它能更好地突出科学研究的客观性,也有助于灵活地平衡句子结构。汉语句子中也有被动句,除了"被"字以外,"由""给""让""为""挨""遭""受到""得以""加以"等词也能表达被动的意思。因此,把英语被动句翻译成汉语时,应根据上下文选择合适的词来体现被动含义,以使句子更通顺流畅。

由于汉语被动句常给人一种消极、被动的感觉,所以汉语主动句的使用频率大大超过被动句。在翻译英语被动句时,大量句子常翻译成汉语主动句,少数句子仍可译成被动句。

1. 英语句子强调被动动作,或者由介词 by 引导的动作主体明确时,可以译成被动句以突出其被动意义。例如:

| Besides voltage, resistance and capacitance, an alternating current is also influenced by inductance. | 除了电压、电阻和电容之外,交流电还受到电感的影响。 |

Unit 6　On-Demand Economy

| This problem has been mitigated now that revisions are saved automatically on many programs, but it has not been solved. | 目前，许多程序自动保存修改的问题虽得以缓解，但尚未得到解决。 |

2. 英语被动语态的主语为无生命的名词，动作主体未出现时，往往可译成汉语的主动句，原句的主语在译文中仍为主语，实际是省略了"被"字的被动句。例如：

| Nuclear power's danger to health, safety and even life itself can be summed up in one word: radiation. | 核能对健康、安全，甚至对生命本身构成的危险可以概括为一个词——辐射。 |
| Refineries are huge "factories" where crude oil is separated into "fractions". | 炼油厂是巨大的工厂，原油在这里分离成各种成分。 |

3. 汉译时，把原句的介词宾语译成主语，相当于行为主体，而把原句主语译成宾语。例如：

| The DNA can be edited by a new gene editing tool, CRISPR. | 新基因编辑工具 CRISPR 可以编辑 DNA。 |
| The numerical data concerned are provided in the next chapter. | 下一章提供了相关的数据资料。 |

4. 根据上下文逻辑增补"人们""有人""大家""我们"等词作主语，并把原句的主语译成宾语。例如：

| In order to explore the moon's surface, rockets were launched again and again. | 为了探测月球的表面，人们一次又一次地发射火箭。 |
| Spanish sage essential oil was found to help enhance memory and stimulate brain function. | 人们发现西班牙鼠尾草精油有助于提高记忆力、激发大脑功能。 |

5. 英语中的某些固定动词短语如 make use of、pay attention to、take measures to、take care of、make efforts to 等用于被动句中（通常施动者未出现）时，往往译成汉语的无主句。例如：

| Measures have been taken to curb industries that over-exploit resources and cause environmental damage. | 已经采取措施遏制过度开发资源以及破坏环境的行业。 |
| Great efforts should be made to promote cooperation on new energy and ecological resource protection. | 应该大力推动新能源和生态资源保护方面的合作。 |

6. 翻译 it 作形式主语的被动句时，可按无主句处理，也可增补"我们""人们""有人"等词作主语，并根据上下文和表达习惯决定是否需要主语。例如：

It is hypothesized that the integration of cognitive psychology and neuroimaging techniques can provide valuable insights into the neural mechanisms underlying human decision-making processes.	假设认知心理学与神经影像技术的结合可以为揭示人类决策过程的神经机制提供有价值的观点。
It is widely understood and accepted that the success of any organization is not solely determined by its leaders, but also by the collective efforts and contributions of all its members.	我们普遍理解并接受的观点是，任何组织的成功不仅仅取决于其领导者，还取决于所有成员的集体努力和贡献。

二、定语从句的翻译

定语从句是一种从属从句，用于修饰主句中的名词或代词，起到进一步限定、描述或说明这个词的作用。通过定语从句，我们可以添加更多的细节，使句子更具丰富性和准确性。因此，定语从句汉译时可采用合译、分译、融合等不同方法。此外，有些定语从句还可起到状语从句的作用，翻译时可根据定语从句与主句之间的关系灵活处理。

1. 当定语从句较短时，可以按照汉语习惯把定语从句译成"……的"，置于被修饰词前面。例如：

They found that among those who took an hour-long brisk walk every day, the effects of the weight-promoting genes were cut in half.	他们发现，在那些每天快走一小时的人中，增胖基因的影响减半。
Artificially intelligent robots, which take wonderfully diverse forms, are responsible for all productive labor.	拥有丰富多样形态的人工智能机器人负责所有的生产性劳动。

2. 当定语从句较长或较复杂时，可采用分译的方法，根据具体情况，将定语从句置于主句前先翻译，或者将定语从句放在主句之后翻译，必要时重复先行词，以符合汉语的习惯。例如：

How to protect our planet, which has been plagued by increasingly severe environmental problems, has become a major concern to the many.	我们的星球受到日益严重的环境问题的困扰，如何保护它已经成为许多人关注的主要问题。
The push to develop more powerful chatbots has led to a race that could determine the next leaders of the tech industry.	推动开发更强大的聊天机器人已经引发了一场竞赛，（这场竞赛）有可能决定科技行业下一任的领军者。

3. 在某些情况下，主句和定语从句之间在语义上存在对比或转折关系，可以用"而""但""可是"这样的连词把这两部分连接起来，主句和定语从句分别译成两个并列分

句。例如：

It pushes food writers, celebrity chefs and some environmentalists to propose answers to the planetary crisis that are even more damaging than the problems they claim to address.	它促使美食作家们、名厨和一些环保主义者提出应对地球危机的办法，但这些办法比他们声称要解决的问题更具破坏性。
The study, which initially hypothesized a positive correlation between income and happiness, unexpectedly revealed a negative association.	该研究最初假设收入与幸福之间存在正相关，但意外地揭示出两者间存在负相关关系。

4. 一些定语从句与主句有非常密切的逻辑关系，语义上可以表示主句发生的原因、结果、目的、时间、条件等。在这些情况下，可以将定语从句翻译成相应的状语从句。例如：

Whether or not vegetarianism should be advocated for adults, it is definitely unsatisfactory for growing children, who need more protein than they can get from vegetable sources.	无论是否应该在成人中提倡素食主义，对成长中的儿童来说，素食肯定是不够好的，因为他们需要的蛋白质远超过从植物性食物中获取的蛋白质。
Camillo Golgi's "black reaction" accidentally solved this problem, which paved the way for experimental observation and the establishment of the Neuron Doctrine.	卡米洛·高尔基的"黑色反应"意外地解决了这个问题，从而为实验观察和神经元学说的建立铺平了道路。
He who breaks the law should be punished.	无论谁犯法都要受到惩戒。
The products that are beautifully packed are not accepted by most consumers.	尽管这些产品包装精美，但大多数顾客还是不接受。

→ Exercises

I. Translate the following sentences into Chinese.

1. The samples were eroded for 6 hours with an ultrasonic cavitation erosion device, and their mass losses were measured.

_____

_____

2. Most of the technology we describe is used within high schools, although it remains restricted to technology programs or peripatetic curricula.

3. It was acknowledged that this project may face hurdles, which might result in the failure of the project if implementation facilitators were not first determined.

4. The selective role of the environment in shaping and maintaining the behavior of the individual is only beginning to be recognized and studied.

5. In the genetic age, ecologists' jobs are made much easier by two things.

II. Translate the following sentences into Chinese.

1. We should be familiar with those signs and symptoms which may be indicative of stroke.

2. Many complications which high blood pressure causes are serious.

3. Several different clinical classifications exist which vary only in details.

Unit 6 On-Demand Economy

4. Most people tend to associate venture capital with so-called "start-up" or "seed investing" where the investment occurs prior to the organization of the company or the development of an actual product.

   _____

   _____

5. Revenge bedtime procrastination is a phenomenon in which people who don't have much control over their daytime life refuse to sleep early in order to regain some sense of freedom during late night hours.

   _____

   _____

Unit 7

Gene Editing: Hope or Disaster?

Part I
Reading

The Future of Medicine: 3D Printers Can Create Human Body Parts

Shelby Rogers & Maia Mulko

① In recent years, updates in 3D printing technologies have allowed medical researchers to print things that were not possible to make using the previous version of this technology, including food, medicine, and even body parts.

② In 2018, doctors from the Ontario Veterinary College 3D printed a **custom titanium** plate for a dog that had lost part of its **skull** after cancer surgery.

③ "By performing these procedures in our animal patients, we can provide valuable information that can be used to show the value and safety of these **implants** for humans", said **veterinary** surgical oncologist Michelle Oblak at the time. "These implants are the next big leap in personalized medicine that allows for every element of an individual's medical care to be specifically **tailored** to their particular needs."

④ And not just for animal patients.

What Is 3D Bioprinting?

⑤ 3D bioprinting is the utilization of 3D printing technologies to **fabricate** body parts. Bioprinters work in a similar way to 3D printers. However, instead of **depositing** materials such as plastic or ceramic, they deposit layers of biomaterial, including living cells, to build complex structures like blood vessels or skin tissue.

⑥ The required cells are taken from a patient and then cultivated. These cells are usually combined with a carrier material or **scaffold**. This carrier is usually a type of biopolymer gel, which acts as a 3D **molecular** scaffold and provides protection for the cells during the printing process. Cells attach to the gel, which is **sturdy** enough to allow printing and flexible enough to allow the flow and **diffusion** of nutrients and the movement of cells. This combination of **encapsulated** cells and biopolymer gels is the bio-ink used by biomedical engineers to create 3D-printed, tissue-like structures.

⑦ Detailed computer designs and models are first made, often based on scans such as magnetic resonance imaging or computerized tomography taken directly from a patient. Precision printer heads then deposit cells and bio-inks exactly where they are needed and, over the course of several hours, an organic object is built up using a large number of very thin layers.

⑧ The cells are kept alive using liquefied nutrients and oxygen during the whole process.

⑨ In the post-printing stage, the structures may be crosslinked with UV light or ionic solutions to make them more stable. Cells are chemically and mechanically stimulated to control the remodeling and growth of tissues. Then, the 3D printed product is put into an **incubator** to allow the cells to grow.

Tendons and Ligaments

⑩ In 2018, biomedical engineers from the University of Utah developed a method for 3D printing **ligaments** and **tendons**. The method involves first taking stem cells from the patient and printing them on a layer of **hydrogel** to form a tendon or ligament. This is allowed to grow **in vitro** in a **culture** before being implanted. However, the process was very complex, because connective tissue is made up of different cells in complex patterns. The team first needed to develop a special printer head that could lay down human cells in the highly controlled manner they require.

⑪ To do this, the team partnered with Utah-based company Carterra, Inc., to develop a specialized printhead that would let them lay down cells in complex patterns. The printhead was then attached to a 3D printer normally used to print antibodies for cancer treatment.

⑫ With this technique, the scientists managed to 3D print stem cells taken from a patient's body fat onto a layer of hydrogel. This hydrogel facilitates cell growth in vitro in a culture, forming either a ligament or tendon in the process.

⑬ The new tissue is then implanted in the damaged area of the patient's body, eliminating the need for additional tissue replacement procedures.

⑭ Replacement tissues for those needing it are often harvested from elsewhere on a patient's body or from a *cadaver*. However, tissue from cadavers runs a high risk of being rejected by the surrounding tissues or of being of poor quality and ineffective.

⑮ Instead, tissues created from the patient's own cells can reduce the *complications* involved with a transplant and speed up the healing process.

Skin Bioprinting and Wound Healing

⑯ 3D bioprinting could also help us say goodbye to skin *grafts* in the near future, as doctors could be able to 3D print new skin for each patient.

⑰ Skin grafting is the transplantation of healthy skin from an animal, a human donor, or the patient's own body to another part of his or her body where the skin is badly damaged. The procedure is commonly used to treat severe wounds, burns, *ulcers*, and infections, or after the removal of skin cancers.

⑱ But the technique involves several risks, from *hemorrhages* and loss of sensitivity to infections, scarring, and rejection.

⑲ This is why scientists from Wake Forest Institute for Regenerative Medicine (WFIRM) are working on a mobile bedside skin bioprinting system that could let doctors print bi-layered skin directly on the patient's wound.

⑳ Meanwhile, in Dublin, scientists from the RCSI University of Medicine and Health Sciences developed a hydrogel scaffold with natural platelet-rich plasma (PRP) that has promising regenerative properties. The compound can be used as a bio-ink to accelerate the wound healing process in 3D printed tissues.

㉑ "Existing literature suggests that while the PRP already present in our blood helps to heal wounds, scarring can still occur," said RCSI Professor Fergal O'Brien. "By 3D printing PRP into a biomaterial scaffold, we can increase the formation of blood vessels while also avoiding the formation of scars, leading to more successful wound healing."

Blood Vessels

㉒　Perhaps the ultimate goal of 3D bioprinting is to assemble functional organs and solve the problem of organ transplantation.

㉓　Currently, there are more than 100,000 people waiting for an organ on the U.S. national transplant waiting list. Roughly 17 of them die each day because they don't receive the organ they need. This is largely due to the lack of donors. Although around 60% of Americans are signed up as donors, organ donation is only possible in 3 out of every 1,000 deaths.

㉔　3D bioprinting of organs could save a lot of lives, but scientists struggle to create the *vascular* structures needed to create *viable* printed organs. All organs, including 3D-printed ones, need an effective, continuous blood supply to prevent the death of the cells and the tissues.

㉕　In October 2021, a team of researchers at Israel's Technion Institute of Technology managed to 3D print blood vessel structures to add a blood supply to tissue implants.

㉖　These structures grew spontaneously after the team implanted endothelial cells from the inner layer of blood vessels in the body in a polymeric *collagen* scaffold.

㉗　However, these are only microvessels that can be used to improve in vitro tissue development—they wouldn't be able to, "feed" a whole organ, and so far, they don't allow the integration of lab-grown tissues into the patient's vascular system.

㉘　This study shows that there's still a long way to go until we can actually 3D print organs on demand. But who knows which techniques can scientists develop to solve this issue in the future?

→ Words and Expressions

custom *adj.* [only before noun] specially designed and made for a particular person 定制的

titanium *n.* a strong light silver-white metal that is used to make aircraft and spacecraft, and is often combined with other metals. It is a chemical element: symbol Ti 钛（金属元素）

skull *n.* the bones of a person's or animal's head 颅骨，头骨

implant *n.* something artificial that is put into someone's body in a medical operation（植入人体中的）移植物，植入物

veterinary *adj.* [only before noun] relating to the medical care and treatment of sick animals 兽医的

tailor *vt.* to make something so that it is exactly right for someone's particular needs or for a particular purpose 定制

fabricate *vt.* to make or produce goods or equipment 制造，生产

deposit *vt.* to put something down in a particular place 放下，放置

scaffold *n.* a supporting framework 支架

molecular *adj.* of, relating to, consisting of, or produced by molecules 分子的；与分子有关的

sturdy *adj.* strong, well-made, and not easily broken 结实的，坚固的

diffusion *n.* the state of being spread out or transmitted especially by contact; the action of diffusing 扩散，传播

encapsulate *vt.* to completely cover something with something else, especially in order to prevent a substance getting out 将……装入胶囊；将……封进内部

incubator *n.* a piece of equipment used to keep eggs or bacteria at the correct temperature for them to develop 细菌培养器；微生物培养器

ligament *n.* a band of strong material in your body, similar to muscle, that joins bones or holds an organ in its place 韧带

tendon *n.* a thick strong string-like part of your body that connects a muscle to a bone 腱

hydrogel *n.* a gel composed usually of one or more polymers suspended in water 水凝胶

in vitro outside the living body and in an artificial environment 在体外

culture *n.* bacteria or cells grown for medical or scientific use, or the process of growing them 培养物

cadaver *n.* a dead human body, especially one used for study 死尸

complication *n.* a medical problem or illness that happens while someone is already ill and makes treatment more difficult 并发症

graft *n.* a piece of healthy skin or bone taken from someone's body and put in or on another part of their body that has been damaged 移植的皮肤（或骨骼等）；移植

ulcer *n.* a sore area on your skin or inside your body that may bleed or produce poisonous substances 溃疡

hemorrhage *n.* a copious or heavy discharge of blood from the blood vessels 大出血

vascular *adj.* relating to the tubes through which liquids flow in the bodies of animals or in plants 血管的

viable *adj.* able to continue to live or to develop into a living thing 能存活的，能生长发育的

collagen *n.* a protein found in people and animals. It is often used in beauty products and treatments to make people look younger and more attractive 胶原，胶原质

➔ Notes

1. **Ontario Veterinary College** 安大略省兽医学院
   加拿大最古老的兽医学院，位于安大略省圭尔夫市的圭尔夫大学校园内。

2. **bio-ink** 生物墨水
   将组织或脏器经过处理去除细胞后生产成的一种"墨水"，可用于3D打印机，用以制造出与实际器官组织极其相似的人造组织。

3. **University of Utah** 犹他大学
   位于美国犹他州的盐湖城，是一所著名的公立研究性大学，于1850年建立。作为该州的旗舰大学，它提供100多个本科专业和90多个研究生学位课程。

4. **Carterra, Inc.** 卡特拉公司
   位于美国犹他州盐湖城的生物技术公司。

5. **Wake Forest Institute for Regenerative Medicine** 维克森林再生医学研究所
   位于美国北卡罗来纳州，是一家将科学发现转化为临床治疗的研究机构。

6. **RCSI (Royal College of Surgeons in Ireland)** 爱尔兰皇家外科医学院
   成立于1784年，是一所位于爱尔兰都柏林市的私立医科大学，学院下分为医学部、物理治疗部和药学部。

7. **platelet-rich plasma** (PRP) 富血小板血浆
   将动物或人的全血经过离心后得到的富含高浓度血小板的血浆，在其中加入凝血酶后可变为胶状物，因此也被称为富血小板凝胶或富血小板白细胞凝胶。

8. Israel's Technion Institute of Technology 以色列理工学院
   一所公立研究型大学，位于以色列海法市，成立于1912年，被誉为中东的麻省理工学院。

→ Reading Skills

Identifying and Understanding Evaluative Language

Evaluative language is a type of language that expresses an opinion or judgement about something or someone. This language can be found in a wide range of contexts, from academic writing and literature to everyday conversation and social media. Being able to identify and understand evaluative language is an important skill for effective communication and critical thinking.

Evaluative language is typically characterized by the use of words that convey positive or negative attitudes towards the subject under discussion. Examples of evaluative language include adjectives such as "good", "bad", "beautiful", "ugly", "interesting", "boring", "impressive", and "disappointing". Evaluative language also includes comparative language, such as "better", "worse", "more", "less", and "most".

One way to identify evaluative language is to look for words that express an opinion or judgement. For example, consider the sentence "By performing these procedures in our animal patients, we can provide valuable information that can be used to show the value and safety of these implants for humans." in Para. 3. In this sentence, the word "valuable" is evaluative language because it expresses a positive opinion about the role of the performance. Similarly, the sentence "However, tissue from cadavers runs a high risk of being rejected by the surrounding tissues or of being of poor quality and ineffective." in Para. 14 uses the evaluative language, such as "poor" and "ineffective", to express a negative opinion about the quality of the tissue from cadavers.

Understanding evaluative language involves more than just identifying it. It also requires analyzing the purpose and intended audience of the language. Evaluative language is often used in persuasive writing, such as advertisements, political speeches, and reviews. In these contexts, evaluative language is used to persuade the audience to adopt a particular viewpoint or take a specific action. Understanding the intended audience is essential for identifying how evaluative language is being used to influence their opinions.

In academic writing, evaluative language is often used to critique or evaluate the quality of research, ideas, and arguments. In this context, evaluative language is used to provide a critical analysis of the subject matter rather than persuade the reader to adopt a particular viewpoint. For instance, look at the sentence "By 3D printing PRP into a biomaterial scaffold, we can increase the formation of blood vessels while also avoiding the formation of scars, leading to more successful wound healing." in Para. 21. The author uses "more successful" to evaluate the advantage of the use of 3D printing PRP into a biomaterial scaffold. Meanwhile, it is important to use evaluative language appropriately in academic writing, for it can be seen as subjective and biased if overused.

In conclusion, identifying and understanding evaluative language is a crucial skill for academic reading and writing. By developing an awareness of evaluative language, we can become more discerning consumers of information and better communicators.

→ Exercises

I. Building Vocabulary

Choose the best word in the box to fill in each blank. Use each word only once and make proper changes where necessary.

molecular	custom	viable	diffusion	spontaneously
sturdy	complication	fabricate	scaffold	deposit

1. The ability of the immune system to generate endlessly diverse _____ receptors also depends on genes that can rearrange and recombine quickly.

2. The digital makeup of the sensor means it is _____ and fast, yet simple and cheap to produce.

3. Perhaps there was a _____ because of some medication she was taking.

4. It was nontoxic and inexpensive, and it had wonderful _____ qualities that the liquids couldn't match.

5. But farming will not remain _____ if the farms are left unmodernized, and most of the farmers lack the financial resources modernization requires.

6. They don't _____ the lights themselves but pass the designs to a smaller manufacturer who in turn may subcontract elements of the manufacture.

7. That suggests the rich are capable of compassion, if somebody reminds them, but do not show it _____.

8. After the lessons on the environment, children _____ much more litter in trash cans, rather than dropping it.

9. These organ regeneration projects use three-dimensional printers to print out a biodegradable _____ and then populate it with stem cells.

10. To create a _____ wireless system, the group had to agree to use proprietary, non-open-source software.

II. Understanding the Text

In this text, evaluative language contributes to the author's critical analysis of 3D bioprinting. Read the text again and fill in the chart below according to his statements.

What are the author's opinions of 3D bioprinting?
(Give examples from the text)

III. Theme Exploration

In recent decades, 3D bioprinting has served several purposes for mankind as a booming technology. For example, it can decrease the use of animals for drug testing as bioprinted tissue can be used to test the effects of drug treatments. Work in groups and discuss other benefits that 3D bioprinting can achieve.

IV. Real-Life Project

Every day, 17 people die waiting for an organ transplant in the United States, according to the Health Resources & Services Administration. And every 10 minutes, another person is added to the waitlist, the agency says. The development of xenotransplantation could, to some extent, solve the problem of insufficient donor organs, and gene editing is expected to well solve the host's rejection of implanted organs.

However, for patients, it is undoubtedly a better choice if they can use the artificial organs developed from their own cells to eliminate transplant rejection. Thus, 3D bioprinting has the potential to be a "game-changer" because it provides an alternative source of organs, which no longer necessitates the need for living or deceased human donation as human organs would be printed on demand. Nevertheless, it also comes with its own set of practical, moral, and legal issues that must be resolved. For example, 3D bioprinting may not be a game-changer for everyone and certainly not for most in its immediate applications because of the high cost of bioprinting self-organs. Please search for relevant information about the challenges of 3D bioprinting and prepare a three-minute presentation about your research results.

Part II
Writing
Methods

1. Functions of the Methods Section

The methods section of a research paper, which usually follows the introduction section, is written to describe the essential details of how the research was conducted. In some research papers, the methods section may also be signaled by other headings such as "Materials and Methods", "Research Design" or "Experimental Procedures". Regardless of the name used, this section is regarded as a crucial part of a research paper because a well-written methods section can perform the following two functions:

First, the information it provides, such as materials, instruments, technology, and other elements related to the research procedure, lays the foundation for the interpretation of the results. Second, the information given in this section can help the readers judge the validity of the research and replicate the experiment to evaluate the reproducibility of the results.

2. Moves in the Methods Section

In terms of structural moves, the methods section is quite variable across disciplines. However, according to style manuals (e.g., *The Publication Manual of the APA*) and studies on the methods sections of published empirical research papers from different disciplines (Peacock, 2011; Cotos et al., 2017), there are some moves (headings of the moves may vary in different disciplines) that commonly appear in the methods sections. These moves include an overview of the research/experiment, experimental location/setting, participants, materials, measures/instruments, research procedures, and data treatment / statistical analysis.

Moves	Functions	Examples
Overview of the research/ Experiments	Restating research purposes, hypotheses or gaps; introducing the overall strategy or the methodological approach	To address these research questions, we developed a self-paced reading task in German in which lexical and syntactic cross-linguistic overlaps in Spanish (L1) and German (L2) were manipulated. In the experimental items, target manipulations focused on the gender of nouns at the lexical level and the relative order of attributive adjectives and nouns in NPs at the syntactic level.
Experimental location/ Setting	Presenting essential characteristics of the research environment such as place, temperature, temporal indicators, and conditions of the research	Naturally gynogenetic blunt snout bream, blunt snout bream and Chinese perch were reared under standard conditions at the Xuefeng Mountain Fish Breed Base (Wugang, Hunan, China). All fish were maintained in three tanks (2 ha and depth 4 m) with suitable density, pH (7.0–8.5), water temperature (22–24 ℃), dissolved oxygen content (5.0–8.0 mg/L) and adequate forage.
Participants	Indicating sample size, types of samples and some basic demographic information of the participants such as age, gender, education level, and ethnicity	The unit of analysis in this study is 86 on-demand, text-based, analytical essays written by L2 students from 7th to 12th grade in a large urban school district in California. Close to 80% of the students in this school district are Latinx, and about 33% are classified either as English Learner (EL) or Reclassified Fluent English Proficient (RFEP) based on 2016–2017 enrollment data.
Materials	Describing the apparatus, equipment, mathematical models, tissue preparations, biological specimens and so on	The standardized mortar described in EN 196-1 [37] was adopted as a cement matrix. The mortar was made of Portland cement, tap water and standardized CEN (Comité Européen de Normalisation) sand.
Measures/ Instruments	Describing the instruments, statistical packages, or measurement equipment used in the study for different purposes	The dynamic simulation software (TRNSYS) is used for the simulations of the proposed energy system described above. This simulation software has been used and validated by Drake Landing Community, Canada for similar applications.

(Continued)

Moves	Functions	Examples
Research procedures	Illustrating how experimental steps were taken, or providing detailed description of various investigative actions and their sequence (for example, how specific data were collected or how variables were identified)	Two lists were created such that each participant saw either the grammatical or ungrammatical version of each of the experimental sentences (1a vs 1b) in addition to the grammatical and ungrammatical filler items. In total, each participant was presented with a total of 48 grammatical and 32 ungrammatical sentences, preceded by five practice sentences to familiarize participants with the task.
Data treatment / Statistical analysis	Specifying how data were analyzed or statistical tests were performed	For this analysis, we dichotomized economic food security as scores 0–2 (high and marginal economic food security) and scores 3–10 (low and very low economic food security).

The table above provides possible moves that can be included in the methods section, but not all of them appear in every paper and in the same sequence. In addition, depending on the discipline, the information focus can be different. For example, papers with qualitative studies rely on data from interviews, so they usually elaborate on participants and coding schemes, while papers in some natural sciences may focus on describing materials used and research procedures. Therefore, it is necessary for novice writers to be reflective about their writing purposes and pay attention to the writing guidelines specific to their own research fields.

3. Verb Tense and Voice in the Methods Section

In terms of linguistic features, simple past tense and passive voice are very common in the methods section. Simple past tense is frequently adopted because research work has already been completed by the time researchers start writing their papers, while the reason for the high frequency of passive voice is that emphasis is put on the research itself rather than who conducted it.

→ Exercises

I. **The following passages are taken from the methods section of a research paper titled "Marketing Capability Development Through Networking—An Entrepreneurial Marketing Perspective". Read the passages carefully and decide which move each passage represents.**

A. A further 15 SMEs (small and medium enterprises) were identified, reaching a total of 28 interviews with entrepreneurs. Our final sample consisted of 20 men and 8 women, with ages ranging from 26 to 57. Their educational background ranged from secondary level to postgraduate degrees. Years in business as entrepreneurs also varied from 2 to 30 years...

B. Thematic analysis, following the six steps outlined by Braun & Clarke (2006) was the main method employed in the analysis of the empirical data collected through the interviews... Initially, each interview was briefly analyzed and summarized individually, with subsequent cross-interview analysis. The second step consisted of generating initial codes, with the aim to identify as many potential themes/patterns as possible (Braun & Clarke, 2006).

C. We rely on qualitative research with a multiple-case exploratory design to address our research questions. This methodology allows in-depth examination of "how" or "why" questions when investigating complex phenomena (Eisenhardt & Graebner, 2007) ... Furthermore, the interactional aspects of networking typically require a qualitative approach (Ngugi et al., 2010, Jack et al., 2004), because networking is a social construct, not a phenomenon with "an objective existence".

D. Prior to data collection, we conducted a pre-test of four pilot interviews with entrepreneurs to develop, test and finalize the interview guide... Entrepreneurs were encouraged to speak freely about their networking activities, as well as about the manner in which they marketed their firms, products and services, and answers were often probed. The interviews lasted on average 80 mins, spanning between 45 and 120 mins, and were conducted face-to-face.

II. Find some published journal papers in your field of research and analyze the methods section based on the following questions. Present your findings to the class.

1. What structural moves are presented in the methods section? In what order are they presented? Which move might be optional or obligatory in your research field?

2. How detailed are these method sections? Are they quite condensed or extended?

3. Are there any citations used in the methods section? If yes, when or for what purposes do authors use each citation?

4. How often is passive voice used? Which tense(s) is more dominant?

Part III
Translating

学术论文研究方法翻译

学术论文的方法部分主要提供研究设计、数据采集和分析方法、实验过程等详细信息，以确保研究可重复和可验证。虽然方法部分具有明显的学科差异性，但在一些典型语步上仍有一些常见的功能句型可为翻译提供参考。下面以方法部分的常见语步为例，讨论这些语步的语言特征和翻译方法。需要注意的是，被动语态在研究方法部分的出现频率相对较高，翻译时视具体情况灵活选用语态。

1. 翻译概述研究方法的句子时，可参考的句型如下：

• This study employed/utilized/adopted X method to…

• X approach was chosen/adopted to investigate/determine…

• X was based on the X framework/model proposed by…

请看下面的例子：

Unit 7 Gene Editing: Hope or Disaster?

| 本研究以 Daniele Di Mitri 等提出的多模态学习分析过程模型为基础，构建了多模态学习分析实证研究框架。 | Based on the process model of multimodal learning analytics proposed by Daniele Di Mitri et al., this study constructed an empirical research framework for multimodal learning analytics. |

2. 翻译描述研究样本的句子时，常见的词有 cohort、subject、sample、participant、criteria、select、include、choose、recruit、consist of、divide 等，可参考的句型如下：

- The cohort was divided into two groups according to...

- A random sample of X was recruited from...

- The initial sample consisted of...

- The subjects were selected on the basis of...

- Criteria for selecting the subjects were as follows:

请看下面的例子：

| 浙江大学现代制造工程研究所以匿名形式进行随机抽样调查，发放问卷80份，回收问卷52份，剔除存在明显错误和缺失的无效问卷，最终有效问卷50份。 | An anonymous random sampling survey was conducted in the Institute of Advanced Manufacturing Engineering in Zhejiang University. A total of 80 questionnaires were distributed, with 52 being collected. After the elimination of the invalid questionnaires with obvious mistakes and omissions, 50 valid questionnaires were finally obtained. |
| 造纸废水的活性污泥样品取自抚顺地区某造纸厂的两个氧化沟（A 沟、B 沟）。 | The activated sludge samples of papermaking wastewater were obtained from two oxidation ditches (ditch A and ditch B) at a paper mill in Fushun. |

3. 翻译描述研究过程的句子时，可以用不定式或 for 短语来表示每个步骤的目的，例如：

- In order to identify X, the participants were asked to...

- For (the purpose of)..., ... were extracted from...

翻译描述具体研究过程的句子时，可采用序列词（sequence word）来表明研究步骤。常见的序列词有 first、after、prior to、following、final、then 等。可参考的句型如下：

- The first/final step in this process was to...

- In the follow-up phase of the study, ...

- Following the treatment, the samples were investigated and stored.

请看下面的例子：

两位研究者先将检索主题设为关键术语：multimodal learning analytics、multi-modal learning analytics，分别在 Web of Science、Science Direct、Springer Link 数据库中进行检索。然后，为确保综述信度，对综述样本进行了二次人工检索。	The two researchers first chose "multimodal learning analytics" and "multi-modal learning analytics" as the key index terms and searched for them in the databases "Web of Science", "Science Direct", and "Springer Link". A second manual search was then conducted on the literature samples to ensure the reliability of the review.
首先将壳聚糖溶液和透明质酸钠溶液混合，然后用恒温蒸干其中的水分得到完全干燥的凝胶薄膜。	Firstly, chitosan solution was mixed with sodium hyaluronate solution, and then the water in them was evaporated at a constant temperature to obtain a completely dry gel film.

4. 翻译描述研究工具的句子时，可参考 "using + instrument" 结构。例如：

- Data were collected using…

- X was conducted/identified using…

- Comparisons between… were made using…

请看下面的例子：

为了验证上述理论分析的准确性，使用 ABAQUS 标准软件进行了数值模拟。	To verify the accuracy of the theoretical analysis, the numerical simulation was conducted using ABAQUS standard software.
基于上述评价系统，使用 UAM（马德里自治大学）语料库标注软件 CorpusTool version 3.3 对语料进行人工标注。	Based on the abovementioned appraisal system, the corpus was manually annotated using UAM (Universidad Autónoma de Madrid) CorpusTool version 3.3.

5. 翻译陈述数据分析方法的句子时，可参考的句型如下：

- Statistical analysis was performed using X software.

- X software was employed / used to / for…

- Independent sample t-tests were conducted to…

请看下面的例子：

Unit 7　Gene Editing: Hope or Disaster?

利用 Image J 软件对少数相的形态和尺寸进行定量分析。采用截线法计算了 α-Al 晶粒和亚晶的尺寸。	Image J software was employed to quantitatively analyze the morphology and size of the minority phase. Line intercept method was used to calculate the sizes of α-Al grains and subgrains.
对于人口统计数据，连续变量采用独立样本 t 检验或 Mann-Whitney 检验（如果呈非正态分布），分类变量则采用卡方检验或 Fisher 精确检验。	For demographic data, independent t-test or Mann-Whitney test (if distribution was nonnormal) was used for continuous variables, and chi-square test or Fisher's exact test was performed for categorical variables.

➜ Exercises

Complete the following English sentences based on the Chinese.

1. 依据研究对象对口腔预防保健知识的了解，将其分成两组。

   _____ according to their knowledge of oral prevention and oral health.

2. 对研究生心理健康状况及影响因素进行了问卷调查。

   _____ on post-graduates' mental health status and the influencing factors.

3. 进行了驾驶模拟研究，使用不同的场景来评估驾驶人对干扰物和车内干预的反应。

   _____ to assess the drivers' response to distractions and in-vehicle interventions in different scenarios.

4. 研究样本包括来自北京、广州、上海和西安四个地区 12 所高校的 3500 名本科生。

   _____ from 12 universities in Beijing, Guangzhou, Shanghai, and Xi'an.

5. 将初始问卷发放给 50 名受访者进行预调查（pre-survey），然后根据预调查结果进行修改并形成最终问卷。

   _____, and the final questionnaire was then formed after the changes and modifications based on the pre-survey results.

Unit 8

Architecture for the Renewable World

Part I
Reading

Daylighting: Here's Why Natural Light Is the Greatest Tool of Modern Architecture

Christopher McFadden

① The use of natural light is one of the most important aspects of architecture because it affects people's well-being, saves energy, and makes environments more comfortable. Of course, natural light was a major source of **illumination** for many until modern times.

② However, after the invention of electrical lighting, **uptake** was rapid because of the benefits it offered, and it was installed into most large structures in a matter of years. Buildings today are designed to let in more natural light in part because of a desire to save energy, as well as a greater understanding of the health benefits of light.

What Is a Daylight System?

③ Daylighting is when direct sunlight and **diffused** skylight are let into a building in a controlled way. This cuts down on the need for electric lighting, which helps reduce the building's use of energy. It is the practice of designing the **placement** of windows, *skylights*, and reflective surfaces to allow sunlight to provide internal lighting.

What Are the Types of Daylighting Systems?

④ Once the building is in the right location, the next major design consideration is the windows themselves.

⑤ The window area needs to find a good balance between letting in light and dealing with thermal issues like heat loss in the winter and heat gain in the summer. Even high-performance **glazings** don't have **insulation** ratings that come close to those of walls for obvious reasons.

⑥ This is very much something of a **trade-off** between the benefits of added daylight (and cost savings) and the additional cost of heating/cooling that may be a consequence. Compared to a regular window **pane**, a high-performance glazing system usually lets in more light and less heat. This makes it possible to use natural light without making the building harder to cool in the summer.

⑦ Another strategy is to install skylights. In daylighting plans, skylights are often used to provide top lighting or let light in from above. The majority of skylights are passive because they feature a clear or diffusing medium (often **acrylic**) that merely enables light to pass through an opening in the roof, despite the fact that skylights can be either passive or active.

⑧ To improve insulation, they frequently include two layers of material too. Active skylights, on the other hand, have a mirror system inside that may follow the sun and direct light into the skylight well. This is meant to make the skylight work better and provide more light. Some of these systems also make an effort to balance cooling loads with daylighting during the summer months.

⑨ Another method is to use something called daylight redirection devices. These move or "bounce" direct beams of sunlight, usually onto the ceiling of a room. Daylight redirection devices move direct beams of sunlight, usually onto the ceiling of a room. These **fixtures** have two purposes: to reduce glare by deflecting direct sunlight away from eye level; and to allow daylight to enter spaces where it might otherwise be difficult to place a window or skylight. Devices that change the path of sunlight usually have one of two shapes: a wide horizontal element or a system of **slats**. Light shelves are commonly used to describe horizontal daylight redirection systems.

What Are Some Advantages of Daylighting for Different Sectors?

Daylighting is great for office spaces.

⑩ Most people who work in an office tend to be under pressure from many directions. For example, they may be engaged in repetitive and boring tasks that can, and will, make them tired after working for a while.

⑪ Natural lighting in the workplace can lead to better health, fewer sick days, more work getting done, lower costs for the office manager, fewer accidents, better mental performance, better sleep, and higher *morale*.

Daylighting is also great for schools and other educational facilities.

⑫ In educational institutions, both professors and students exhibit certain behaviors that are influenced by the amount of natural light in the classrooms.

⑬ According to a 1998 study titled "Benefits of Natural Daylighting", higher student and instructor attendance, greater achievement rates, decreased weariness, improved student health, and enhancement factors of general student development are among the benefits of natural daylighting.

⑭ Natural lighting in schools has also been linked to physical growth, a good mood throughout the day, and higher levels of alertness and activity in students.

Daylighting has many benefits for the retail sector too.

⑮ Allowing natural light inside stores has become increasingly popular recently because it improves the store's *ambiance*, boosts sales, makes the shopping experience more pleasant, draws consumers in, and enhances color rendering.

⑯ It has been demonstrated that natural light not only makes customers feel more welcome but also makes the store appear cleaner, brighter, and more open.

⑰ Retailers such as Wal-Mart, Target, and Recreational Equipment Incorporated (REI) in Seattle, Washington; Lamb's Thriftway Store in Portland, Oregon; and others have noted the advantages of natural lighting inside the store.

Daylighting helps boost recovery and well-being in hospitals.

⑱ In hospitals, the patient's mental health is the most crucial aspect, and allowing for natural light and air has been shown to improve patients' mental condition and speed up their recovery. The mental and physical burden on patients, doctors, and nurses can be decreased in hospitals with sufficient natural illumination.

⑲ This has also made the relationship between the doctor and patient better and helped patients avoid depression or psychological stress after surgery. *Anecdotally*, an abundance of natural light may help people feel more spiritual, more open, and freer.

There are benefits for the industry as well.

⑳ Industrial settings are typically related, to a large extent, to repetitive physical labor. Architects previously designed many industrial structures without many windows in order to keep dust out, but many people who worked in these windowless industrial settings suffered from problems like increased ***capillary permeability***, ***inflammation***, less white cell activity, and more ***catarrhal*** infections and colds.

㉑ Maximizing the use of natural light within a building is a great way to reduce energy costs and make a space more welcoming for human beings. This has been shown to increase sales and workforce productivity and even improve building users' moods and overall mental health.

㉒ While there are also downsides, attention to detail when developing a daylight strategy really does ***pay dividends*** in the end.

→ Words and Expressions

illumination *n.* lighting provided by a lamp, light, etc. 光亮；照明

uptake *n.* the act of using, participating in, adopting, or taking advantage of an available product, service, opportunity, etc.（对现有东西的）使用，利用，应用

diffuse *v.* to make light shine less brightly by spreading it in many directions（使光）模糊，漫射，漫散

placement *n.* the act of placing something somewhere（对物件的）安置，放置

skylight *n.* a window in the roof of a building（房顶的）天窗

glazing *n.* glass that has been used to fill windows 嵌装玻璃，玻璃窗

insulation *n.* the act of protecting something with a material that prevents heat, sound, electricity, etc.; the materials used for this 隔热，绝缘；绝缘材料

trade-off *n.* a balance between two opposing things that you are willing to accept in order to achieve something 平衡，协调

pane *n.* a single sheet of glass in a window（一片）窗玻璃

acrylic *n.* 丙烯酸材料

fixture *n.* a piece of equipment that is fixed inside a house or building 固定装置

slat *n.* a thin narrow flat strip especially of wood or metal 板条，狭条

morale *n.* the level of confidence and positive feelings that people have, especially people who work together, who belong to the same team, etc. 士气，精神面貌

ambiance *n.* the qualities and character of a particular place and the way these make you feel 氛围，周围环境

anecdotally *adv.* 传闻地；逸事地；趣闻地

capillary *n.* the smallest type of blood vessel (=tube carrying blood) in the body 毛细血管；毛细管

permeability *n.* the quality of allowing a liquid or gas to pass through 渗透性

inflammation *n.* swelling and pain in part of your body, which is often red and feels hot 发炎，炎症

catarrhal *adj.* 鼻黏膜炎的

pay dividends to produce great advantages or profits 有所收获，产生效益

➔ Notes

1. **color rendering** 显色性；色彩渲染
   光源对物体的显色能力称为显色性，它是评价照明质量的重要方面。光源的显色性通常用显色指数（color rendering index，CRI）来表征，其取值范围从 0 到 100，CRI 值越高，光源的显色性越好。

2. **Wal-Mart** 沃尔玛百货有限公司
   美国世界性连锁企业，由零售业传奇人物山姆·沃尔顿于 1962 年在美国阿肯色州成立。1996 年沃尔玛进入中国，在深圳开设了第一家沃尔玛购物广场和山姆会员商店。

3. **Target** 塔吉特公司
   美国零售百货集团，1961 年成立。2022 年《财富》美国 500 强排行榜发布，Target 公司位列第 32 名。

4. **Recreational Equipment Incorporated** (REI) 安伊艾户外用品零售组织
   美国专业户外和运动产品品牌，1938 年由 Lloyd 和 Mary Anderson 创建于华盛顿州的西雅图，是美国也是全球最大的户外用品连锁零售组织。

5. **Lamb's Thriftway Store**
   美国平价二手店，位于俄勒冈州波特兰市，商品以便宜实惠著称。

Unit 8   Architecture for the Renewable World

→ **Reading Skills**

Making Inferences

An inference is an idea or conclusion drawn from evidence and the use of reasoning. Making inferences is regarded as an essential skill in reading comprehension. Writers sometimes do not state everything explicitly and directly in their writing, so it is necessary for readers to read between the lines and determine the implied information. For example, when reading the sentence "Tony's face turned red and he started to yell, balling his hands up into shaking fists", readers can deduce Tony's anger from the evidence of his red face, yelling, and clenched fists although the writer does not directly state that Tony is angry. By making good inferences on the basis of textual evidence and their prior knowledge, proficient readers can form interpretations, make critical judgements, and draw conclusions about what they have read, thus gaining a comprehensive and deep understanding of a text.

There are some strategies for making reasonable inferences. First, it is important to find the clues and hints authors leave behind. One way that readers make inferences is to decipher the meaning of an unknown word by using context clues such as transitional words or connective words, synonym or antonym clues, or a direct definition of the word. For instance, the meaning of the word "fixture" in Para. 9 can be inferred from the referential pronoun "these" and the synonym "devices". Contextual clues can also help determine the attitude a writer holds towards something. Descriptive words, modality words, and sometimes even a single adverb imply a writer's feelings and intentions. For example, in Para. 7, the adverb "merely" conveys a negative tone towards "passive skylights", although the information that passive skylights are not good is not directly stated. In addition to contextual clues, readers may draw on general knowledge of the world to fill in missing details and fully understand a text. For this text about daylighting, prior knowledge about architecture, lighting systems and various public buildings undoubtedly plays an important part in improving readers' comprehension.

> In a word, making inferences while reading is an active process that gets readers highly engaged. By reading between the lines and connecting the new information with existing knowledge, readers can go beyond the surface level and more thoroughly understand a text.

→ Exercises

I. Building Vocabulary

Choose the best word in the box to fill in each blank. Use each word only once and make proper changes where necessary.

| placement | ambiance | insulation | diffuse | fixture |
| illumination | inflammation | dividend | trade-off | morale |

1. When planning the _____ of the swimming pool, the architects carefully studied the path of the sun.

2. As workplaces become increasingly distributed, leaders will need to take into account how the arrangement of teams will impact productivity and, more importantly, what it will do to long-term employee _____ and well-being.

3. Chronic _____ is associated with major illnesses like heart disease and various cancers.

4. Finding moments to maintain hobbies and interests amidst the trials of life can pay great _____ in terms of achieving the goal of wellness.

5. If you don't want the foosball table to be a permanent _____ in your space, there are foldable and portable options available.

6. He switched on the torch, but directed it upward so that there was only _____ light on the forest floor.

7. There is a(n) _____ between the benefits of the drug and the risk of side effects.

8. Night _____ is so dim that stars are visible from the center of the city.

9. Each place we visit has its own particular look, character, and _____.

10. _____ is something which is put on or around a container, pipe, or vessel to prevent loss of heat.

II. Understanding the Text

Discuss the following questions by using the reading skill of making inferences.

1. What can you infer from the title "Daylighting: Here's Why Natural Light Is the Greatest Tool of Modern Architecture"?
2. What can you infer about the writer's opinion on natural light and electrical light from Paras. 1 and 2?
3. What does "trade-off" in Para. 6 suggest according to the context?
4. What can you infer about these people's working condition from Para. 10?
5. What associations do you have with the sentence "…both professors and students exhibit certain behaviors that are influenced by the amount of natural light in the classrooms." in Para. 12?

III. Theme Exploration

Daylighting is widely used in modern buildings to create a more sustainable living environment. Many public buildings, such as shopping malls, libraries, and train stations, have benefited from the practice of daylighting design. However, if a daylighting program is not properly executed, it can also produce unfavorable results. Please work in groups and discuss the problems and challenges that daylighting systems may encounter.

IV. Real-Life Project

According to this text, the term "daylighting" refers to architectural design that brings natural light into buildings. Daylighting is often associated with numerous positive outcomes in building design such as reduced energy consumption, improved health, and enhanced employee performance. Therefore, it's highly desirable in people's lives. Effective use of daylighting and connection to nature are important criteria for high-performance or green buildings. In recent years, some amazing buildings have emerged that utilize daylight in innovative ways. Please search for relevant information and prepare to introduce one or two real-life examples of green buildings in class.

Part II
Writing

Results and Discussion

Writing guidebooks (Cargill & O'Connor, 2009; Swales & Feak, 2012) and academic papers on research article structures (Peacock, 2002; Lin & Evans, 2012; Gong & Barlow, 2022) indicate that disciplinary variations also exist in the results and discussion sections. In some journals, the results section is required to be presented separately from the discussion section, while in others, the two are written in a combined way. Results and discussion play different roles in research papers. In general, the results section is more descriptive (focusing on facts), and the discussion section is more interpretive (focusing on points or claims). Specifically speaking, the results section summarizes and presents the findings of a study objectively, while the discussion section interprets or analyzes the findings and makes claims, thus shedding light on the study's research questions or hypotheses. For instance, writers may describe the correlation between variables in the results section but deal with the causes of the correlation in the discussion section. Additionally, the discussion section is normally the place for authors to state the strengths and possible weaknesses of their research outcomes, compare present findings with previous findings, and suggest gaps for future research.

1. Structure of the Results Section

When writing the results section, some writers may start with a brief introduction to connect the results with the research question(s), bringing the readers' attention back to the purpose of the research and also creating a smooth flow of information, but most will choose to present the findings directly from the very beginning. The findings are usually reported in both written text and non-textual forms such as tables, graphs, figures, or other images. The functions of text are to describe and clarify the visual information, as is shown in the following example:

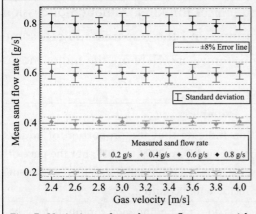

Fig. 7. Variation of sand mass flow rate with respect to conveying air velocity

In experiment-3, Fig. 7 presents the real-time monitored calculation (Eq. (4)) results that sand mass flow rate varies with conveying air velocity.

Standard deviation is applied to reveal the volatility of minimum and maximum sand mass flow rate, and the volatility is caused by different sand size. All of these measured sand mass flow rates are within ±8% of the true value (as indicated by the error bounds highlighted by dotted red lines). These experimental results are given to support the theoretical formula computing results.

The results section states the findings in a systematic way. First, tables or figures should be numbered according to the order in which they are mentioned. When describing the visuals, authors are suggested to start with location elements and summary statements, such as "Table 1 shows the most common sources of computer viruses in U.S. business", followed by the description of specific findings from the visuals. Second, instead of covering all the data shown in the visuals, the results section should highlight crucial findings most relevant to the research under investigation, such as representative data, recurring patterns, regularities, or variables that have an effect (positive or negative). Some guidebooks also suggest mentioning possible unexpected findings, even if they do not support the research hypothesis. Third, to increase clarity, the results section can be divided into several subsections based on the research questions or the key themes that emerged from the data analyzed.

2. Verb Tenses in the Results Section

Both past tense and present tense can be found in the results section. The past tense is usually used to describe the completed experiments and report the findings obtained. However, when directing readers to a specific table, figure, or graph and describing the visual information, writers tend to use the present tense.

3. Structure of the Discussion Section

The discussion section is regarded as the most difficult section to compose because it involves both logical writing and logical thinking. Although discussion sections will vary depending on the discipline and the research subject, some common moves can still be found to create a framework. Here are the major moves and corresponding examples:

Moves	Examples
Summary or review of the key findings	The results of this investigation indicate that the proportion of adults consuming chickpeas more than doubled from 2003 to 2018, but the pace of growth slightly slowed in later years. Chickpea consumption is more prevalent among individuals with higher socioeconomic status...
Comments on the findings (e.g., explaining the results; making claims; relating the new findings to those of previous studies; contribution of the present study)	There are several reasons why chickpea consumption may contribute to or be associated with an overall healthy diet. First, chickpeas are a rich source of dietary fiber... Second, our analysis indicated that chickpea consumers also... Finally, the higher intakes of whole grains... may be due to complementary food practices. (**Explaining the results**) When comparing the results of our analysis to a previous analysis of legume consumption in the United States, there are a few key differences. First, Perera et al. [16] reported that the frequency of legume... declined from 18.5% in 2011 to 13.7% in 2014, whereas we observed an upward trend of... from 2003 to 2018. (**Relating the new findings to those of previous studies**) A major strength of this analysis was the use of a large, nationally representative sample. In addition, our analyses considered specific nutrients... and... to provide a comprehensive view of dietary intake in relation to chickpea consumption. Lastly, our analyses reflect the nutrient density of the diet... (**Contribution of the present study**)
Limitations of the research	A limitation of this study is that the dietary intake data were based on 2 nonconsecutive 24-h dietary recalls; thus, habitual intake may not have been captured...
Suggestions for future research	Future research should investigate the perception of chickpeas and barriers to intake among nonconsumers.

4. Verb Tenses in the Discussion Section

Both past tense and present tense are used in the discussion section. The past tense is generally used to restate the research purpose(s) and summarize the findings, whereas the present tense is adopted to interpret the results, make comparisons, describe the limitations, and make recommendations for future research. It is worthwhile to note that when interpreting research findings and making claims about certain research results, many authors would choose hedges, such as modal auxiliaries and words expressing possibilities, to express their tentativeness and cautiousness (Yang, 2013).

→ Exercises

I. The materials below are taken from a research paper titled "Nonlinearity and Inter- and Intra-Individual Variability in the Extent of Engagement in Self-Reflection and Its Role in Second Language Writing: A Multiple-Case Study". Read them carefully and finish the following two tasks.

1. Read the excerpt from the results section and discuss how the author deals with the data in Fig.1. What suggestions do you have for the description of chronological data in figures or graphs?

| Fig. 1 shows the trajectory of the EESR index for the group data. A gradual increase can be observed between data points 1 and 5. However, at data point 6 the EESR index dropped, but then it increased again at data point 7. The EESR index was 0.27 at data point 1 which means that the participants engaged in self-reflection in only 1 and half of the categories (vocabulary, grammar, structure, genre, and general). In contrast, at data points 5 and 7, the EESR index was 0.80 which means that the participants engaged in self-reflection in four out of the five categories. | 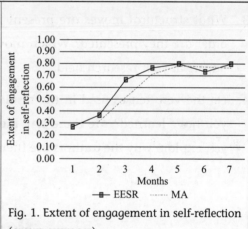
Fig. 1. Extent of engagement in self-reflection (group averages) |

2. Read the following excerpt from the discussion section and decide what function(s) each sentence performs.

❶The participants became cognitively more engaged in self-reflection and tended to provide self-generated feedback in more areas (e.g., vocabulary, grammar) over the seven months. ❷The increase in the EESR index implies that the six participants tended to become more self-regulated L2 writers. ❸The increase in self-regulatory processes is not surprising since Nitta and Baba (2018) also found that one of their two focal learners tended to engage more in self-regulation over time. ❹Likewise, Teng and Zhang (2020) also found that learners who received self-regulated learning strategies-based writing instruction used strategies more actively than learners in the control group. ❺However, Teng and Zhang's (2020) study could not reveal the dynamics of self-regulation. ❻Conversely, in this study the dynamics of self-reflection or self-regulation was explored by showing the nonlinearity of the EESR index.

II. Find some published journal papers in your field of research and locate the results sections and discussion sections. Analyze these sections based on the following questions. Present your findings to the class.

1. How are the two sections structured? Are they combined, written separately or presented in other ways?

2. How do the authors report their research findings? Do they use visual aids? What roles do the visual aids play?

3. What structural moves are present in the results/discussion sections? In what order are they presented? Which move(s) might be optional or obligatory in the papers in your research field?

4. Do the verb tenses used in the results/discussion section follow the conventions you have learned? Are there any modal auxiliaries used in the two sections? If yes, explain why the authors use them.

Part III
Translating

学术论文研究结果和讨论翻译

一、学术论文研究结果的翻译

学术论文研究结果是整篇论文中至关重要的部分，常借助图表、图像或其他可视化手段来呈现研究数据，并通过文字对数据信息进行说明。本部分主要介绍图表及其数据描述相关句子的英译。

Unit 8　Architecture for the Renewable World

1. 由于学科背景差异，学术论文中会出现不同类型的图表，如表格、饼图、柱状图和折线图等。这些图表在英文中常对应不同的词，学术论文中用得较多的是 table、figure、chart。常见的图表类型及对应的英文列举如下：

行列表	table	图像/图表	figure
柱状图	bar chart	饼状图	pie chart
折线图	line chart	树状图	tree chart / diagram
示意图	diagram	散点图	scatter plot/diagram
矩阵图	matrix diagram	金字塔图	pyramid diagram
平面图	floor plan	流程图	flow chart

2. 图表标题的英译与论文标题的英译类似，通常由名词短语构成，不宜用句子或动词短语。一般可以先确定一个词作为中心名词，再用其余的词来修饰、限定这个中心名词。图表中包括表头在内的各部分名称也一般用名词或名词短语来翻译。以下为某一表格信息的中英文对比：

表 1　手机使用及依赖的性别差异
Table 1　Gender Differences in Smartphone Use and Dependence

变量 Variables	范围 Range	总体 （N=2298） Population （N=2298）		女生（n=1180） Females （n=1180）		男生（n=1108） Males （n=1108）		t
		M	SD	M	SD	M	SD	
使用时长 Duration of use	1~6	3.05	1.42	2.99	1.40	3.11	1.44	−2.061*
使用频率 Frequency of use	1~6	3.57	1.47	3.53	1.45	3.61	1.51	−1.243
手机效能 Smartphone performance	1~5	3.25	1.11	3.12	1.11	3.38	1.10	−5.707***
手机依赖 Smartphone dependence	1~5	1.87	0.80	1.84	0.79	1.91	0.81	−2.158*
睡前使用 Smartphone use before sleep	1~5	2.20	0.88	2.23	0.89	2.16	0.87	2.061*

注：*$p<0.05$；***$p<0.001$；10 位参与者没有报告自己的性别。
Note: *$p<0.05$; ***$p<0.001$; Ten participants did not report their gender.

3. 对图表的描述常涉及概述图表主要信息、描述显著性数据或趋势、总结或陈述主要研究结果等内容。

（1）翻译概述图表主要信息的句子时，可以参考的常见句型如下：

- Table X shows/illustrates/demonstrates/presents/provides/compares/summarizes...

- As shown in Figure X / As can be seen from the pie chart, ...

- It can be seen from Table X that...

- The results of... are shown/displayed/presented/summarized in Table X.

请看下面的例子：

英语学习动机自我系统三个层面对动机调控策略的影响效应见表3。	Table 3 shows the effects of the three components of English learning motivational self-system on motivational regulation strategies.
表3总结了不同太阳能利用水平地区的重要社会经济变量，以及它们对这些地区太阳能利用情况的影响。	Table 3 provides a summary of the significant socio-economic variables for different solar-levelled regions, along with their influences on the solar uptake in those regions.

（2）翻译描述图表内突出数据或趋势的句子时，可以参考的常见句型如下：

- What stands out in the chart is the growth/dominance of...

- In Fig. X, there is a clear trend of decreasing in...

- As the table shows, there is a significant difference between group X and group Y.

- From this data, it can be seen that X resulted in the lowest/highest value of...

请看下面的例子：

如表6所示，工科库中立场标记词块的出现总频次显著高于医学库（1504:1291），但医学库中模糊限制语的使用频次反而是工科库的两倍多（388:167）。	As shown in Table 6, the occurrences of stance markers in the engineering database are far more frequent than those in the medical database (1504:1291), however, the occurrences of hedges in the medical database are more than twice those in the engineering database (388: 167).
表1呈现出一个明显趋势，即南川区的非私营部门员工人数在2012年左右开始波动，总体稳定，并小幅上升。	In Table 1, there is a clear trend that the number of non-private sector employees in Nanchuan District began to fluctuate around 2012 and was generally stable, with a slightly rising trend.

（3）翻译总结或陈述主要结果的句子时，可以参考的句型如下：

• The results, as shown in Table X, indicate that...

• A positive correlation was found between X and Y / X is positively correlated with Y.

• There was no evidence that X has an influence on...

• No statistically significant difference was observed/found between X and Y.

请看下面的例子：

表 4 提供的估计结果还表明，学前教育对青少年在校表现的影响会因为学科的不同而产生一定的差异。	The estimation results presented in Table 4 also indicate that the impact of preschool education on adolescents' academic performance varies with academic disciplines.
结果如表 3 所示，可以看出：实验组学生的阅读倾向性、自觉性、时长性均与翻译成绩显著相关。	The results, as shown in Table 3, indicate that students' reading tendency, self-consciousness, and reading duration in the experimental group are significantly correlated with their translation performance.

二、学术论文讨论的翻译

汉语学术论文的讨论部分在内容和结构上与英语论文基本相似，但有些汉语论文将研究不足和建议放在了专门的结论部分。本部分不涉及两者在篇章组织上的差异，主要介绍一些常用句子的翻译。

1. 对研究结果进行解释，分析产生结果的原因时，语气可能会比较谨慎，翻译时可参考以下句型：

• X *could* be attributed to...

• It *seems possible* that these results *are due to*...

• There are two *likely* causes for the differences between...

• These relationships *may partly* be explained by...

• *A possible* explanation for this might be...

请看下面的例子：

本研究还发现，尽管显性教学的即时效果比隐性教学更好，但显性教学组的延时后测成绩出现明显下滑，而隐性教学组的延时后测成绩不降反升……造成这一结果的一个原因可能是学习者在两种教学条件下的信息加工方式不同。	This study also found that although explicit instruction resulted in more favorable immediate outcomes compared with implicit instruction, the delayed post-test scores of the explicit instruction group saw a significant decline, while those of the implicit instruction group showed an increase instead of a decrease... One reason for this result could be that learners adopted different information processing approaches under the two instructional circumstances.

2. 基于结果分析提出观点时，表达既要实事求是，又要适当留有余地，因此翻译时可结合观点的确定性程度选择恰当的词，例如：坚信观点的真实性，可选用 prove、demonstrate；而带有推测意味时，可选用 imply、suggest、infer。

- These findings/results *suggest* that...

- In general, therefore, it *seems* that...

- According to these data, we *can infer* that...

请看下面的例子：

此外，研究证实羟基自由基（HO·）是微生物降解 EE2 的主要活性物质。	Furthermore, it had been demonstrated that hydroxyl radicals (HO·) was the main active substance responsible for the microbial degradation of EE2.
这些结果表明，同时控制 NOx 和 VOCs 有利于削减臭氧。	These results imply that concurrent control of both NOx and VOCs would benefit in ozone reductions.

3. 翻译未来研究启示或建议的句子时，可参考的常用句型如下：

- Future research/studies/investigations need(s) to be conducted to...

- Future investigation into X is strongly recommended.

- Further research should be undertaken to...

- A reasonable approach to tackle this issue could be to...

请看下面的例子：

Unit 8 Architecture for the Renewable World

| 然而，在污染物微生物降解过程中，DOM 与铁矿物的相互作用机制仍需进一步研究。 | However, future research should be undertaken to investigate the mechanism of interaction between DOM and iron minerals in the microbial degradation of pollutants. |

→ Exercises

Translate the following sentences into English.

1. 本文认为，应该加强对中国法律文化典籍的系统研究，归纳和整理出这些典籍中能够体现中国国家法律形象的积极、正面的篇章和话语。

2. 从表 4 中的数据可以看出，汉语学习动机对媒介使用频率和媒介信息源具有显著影响。

3. 结果如表 1 所示，利用超分辨网络（super-resolution network）预测出的图片质量较高，达到了我们的预期效果。

4. 从以上估计结果可以看出，西部地区的经济内循环指数（internal economic circulation index）受到市场经济、开放、城乡融合等制度因素的影响比较小，这可能与西部地区整体的制度发展水平比较低有关，而在东中部地区，影响较为显著。

5. 本研究没有考虑在线学习环境中学生的个体差异，如先前知识或动机等对学生成绩的影响。

Bibliography

American Psychological Association. (2020). *Publication Manual of the American Psychological Association* (7th ed.). https://doi.org/10.1037/0000165-000

Bailey, S. (2014). *Academic Writing: A Handbook for International Students* (4th ed.). London: Routledge.

Cargill, M., & O'Connor, P. (2009). *Writing Scientific Research Articles: Strategy and Steps*. Oxford: Wiley-Blackwell.

Cargill, M., & O'Connor, P. (2013). *Writing Scientific Research Articles: Strategy and Steps* (2nd ed.). Oxford: Wiley-Blackwell.

Cheng, S. W., Kuo. C. W., & Kuo, C. H. (2012). Research article titles in applied linguistics. *Journal of Academic Language and Learning, 6*(1): A1–A14.

Cotos, E., Huffman, S., & Link, S. (2017). A move/step model for methods sections: Demonstrating rigour and credibility. *English for Specific Purposes, 46*: 90–106.

Day, R. A. (1998). *How to Write and Publish a Scientific Paper* (5th ed.). Phoenix: Oryx Press.

Doykova, I. T. (2016). Title structures in research articles. 10th Jubilee International Scientific Conference "The Power of Knowledge", Agia Triada, Greece.

Galvan, J. L., & Galvan, M. (2017). *Writing Literature Reviews: A Guide for Students of the Social and Behavioral Sciences* (7th ed.). New York: Routledge.

Gong, H., & Barlow, M. (2022). A corpus-based analysis of research article macrostructure patterns. *Journal of English for Academic Purposes, 58*, 101138. https://doi.org/10.1016/j.jeap.2022.101138

Hyland, K. (2018). *Academic Writing English*. Shanghai: Shanghai Foreign Language Education Press.

Hyland, K., & Zou, H. (2022). Titles in research articles. *Journal of English for Academic Purposes, 56*, 101094. https://doi.org/10.1016/j.jeap.2022.101094

Kanoksilapatham, B. (2015). Distinguishing textual features characterizing structural variation in research articles across three engineering sub-discipline corpora. *English for Specific Purposes, 37*: 74–86.

Lin, L., & Evans, S. (2012). Structural patterns in empirical research articles: A cross-disciplinary study. *English for Specific Purposes, 31*(3): 150–160.

Nagano, L. R. (2015). Research article titles and disciplinary conventions: A corpus study of eight disciplines. *Journal of Academic Writing, 5*(1): 133–144.

Newmark, P. (2001). *A Textbook of Translation*. Shanghai: Shanghai Foreign Language Education Press.

Oliver, P. (2012). *Succeeding with Your Literature Review: A Handbook for Students*. Berkshire: McGraw-Hill Education.

Peacock, M. (2002). Communicative moves in the discussion section of research articles. *System, 30*(4): 479–497.

Peacock, M. (2011). The structure of methods sections in research articles across eight disciplines. *Asian ESP Journal, 7*: 99–124.

Swales, J. M. (1990). *Genre Analysis: English in Academic and Research Settings*. Cambridge: Cambridge University Press.

Swales, J. M., & Feak, C. B. (2012). *Academic Writing for Graduate Students: Essential Tasks and Skills* (3rd ed.). Ann Arbor: University of Michigan Press.

Wallwork, A. (2016). *English for Writing Research Papers*. Boston: Springer.

Yang, Y. (2013). Exploring linguistic and cultural variations in the use of hedges in English and Chinese scientific discourse. *Journal of Pragmatics, 50*(1): 23–36.

史文霞.（2012）.学术论文写作与发表.西安：西安交通大学出版社.

Sources of Sample Texts

Agbaglo, E., & Fiadzomor, P. (2021). Genre analysis of abstracts of empirical research articles published in *TESOL Quarterly*. *Journal of English Language Teaching and Applied Linguistics, 3*(7): 1–13.

Begley, S. (2011, Feb., 27). The science of making decisions. *Newsweek*.

Bonfim, G. H. C., Medola, F. O., & Paschoarelli, L. C. (2016). Correlation among cap design, gripping technique and age in the opening of squeeze-and-turn packages: A biomechanical study. *International Journal of Industrial Ergonomics*, 54, 178–183.

Carissimi, M. C., Creazza, A., & Colicchia, C. (2023). Crossing the chasm: Investigating the relationship between sustainability and resilience in supply chain management. *Cleaner Logistics and Supply Chain*, 7, 100098. https://doi.org/10.1016/j.clscn.2023.100098

Chaudhuri, A., Subramanian, N., & Dora, M. (2022). Circular economy and digital capabilities of SMEs for providing value to customers: Combined resource-based view and ambidexterity perspective. *Journal of Business Research*, 142, 32–44.

Chen, A., et al. (2023). Be a good speaker in livestream shopping: A speech act theory perspective. *Electronic Commerce Research and Applications*, 61, 101301. https://doi.org/10.1016/j.elerap.2023.101301

Bibliography

Cores, D., Brea, V. M., & Mucientes, M. (2021). Short-term anchor linking and long-term self-guided attention for video object detection. *Image and Vision Computing*, 110, 104179. https://doi.org/10.1016/j.imavis.2021

Desolda, G., Ferro, L. S., Marrella, A., Catarci, T., & Costabile, M. F. (2021). Human factors in phishing attacks: A systematic literature review. *ACM Computing Surveys (CSUR)*, 54(8): 1–35.

Denning, P. J., & Denning, D. E. (2020). Dilemmas of artificial intelligence. *Communications of the ACM*, 63(3): 22–24.

Didehbani, N., Allen, T., Kandalaft, M., Krawczyk, D., & Chapman, S. (2016). Virtual reality social cognition training for children with high functioning autism. *Computers in Human Behavior*, 62, 703–711.

Dung, L., Wang, S., & Wu, Y. (2018). A multiple random feature extraction algorithm for image object tracking. *Journal of Signal and Information Processing*, 9(1): 63–71.

Elshawi, R., Sherif, Y., Al-Mallah, M., & Sakr, S. (2021). Interpretability in healthcare: A comparative study of local machine learning interpretability techniques. *Computational Intelligence*, 37(4), 12410. https://doi.org/10.1111/coin.12410

Gkinko, L., & Elbanna, A. (2023). Designing trust: The formation of employees' trust in conversational AI in the digital workplace. *Journal of Business Research*, 158, 113707. https://doi.org/10.1016/j.jbusres.2023.113707

Gliga, G., & Evers, N. (2023). Marketing capability development through networking—An entrepreneurial marketing perspective. *Journal of Business Research*, 156, 113472. https://doi.org/10.1016/j.jbusres.2022.113472

Gruhler, K., & Schiller, G. (2023). Grey energy impact of building material recycling—A new assessment method based on process chains. *Resources, Conservation and Recycling Advances*, 18, 200139. https://doi.org/10.1016/j.rcradv.2023.200139

Haidar, Z. A., & Al-Shaalan, A. M. (2018). Reliability evaluation of renewable energy share in power systems. *Journal of Power and Energy Engineering*, 6(9), 40–47.

He, H., et al. (2024). Dissolved organic matter accelerates microbial degradation of 17 alpha-ethinylestradiol in the presence of iron mineral. *Journal of Environmental Sciences*, 139, 364–376.

Higginbotham, G., & Reid, J. (2019). The lexical sophistication of second language learners' academic essays. *Journal of English for Academic Purposes*, 37, 127–140.

Hsieh, L. F., Chuang, C. C., Tseng, C. S., Wei, C. C., & Hsu, W. C. (2014). Combined home exercise is more effective than range-of-motion home exercise in patients with ankylosing spondylitis: A randomized controlled trial. *BioMed Research International*, 5, 398190. http://dx.doi.org/10.1155/2014/398190

Hu, H., Zhu, Y, Li, S., & Li, Z. (2021). Effects of green energy development on population growth and employment: Evidence from shale gas exploitation in Chongqing, China. *Petroleum Science*, 18(5): 1578–1588.

Joo, W., et al. (2020). Metasurface-driven OLED displays beyond 10,000 pixels per inch. *Science*, 370(6515): 459–463.

Jung, C. & Schindler, D. (2023). Efficiency and effectiveness of global onshore wind energy utilization. *Energy Conversion and Management*, 280, 116788. https://doi.org/10.1016/j.enconman.2023.116788

Katzer, J. & Skoratko, A. (2022). Using 3D printed formworks for the creation of steel fiber reinforced concrete-plastic columns. *Construction and Building Materials*, 337, 127586. https://doi.org/10.1016/j.conbuildmat.2022.127586

Klassen, R., Kolb, N., Hopp, H., & Westergaard, M. (2022). Interactions between lexical and syntactic L1–L2 overlap: Effects of gender congruency on L2 sentence processing in L1 Spanish–L2 German speakers. *Applied Psycholinguistics*, 43(6): 1221–1256.

Koleva, M. N., & Vulkov, L. G. (2018). Fast computational approach to the delta Greek of non-linear black-scholes equations. *Journal of Computational and Applied Mathematics*, 340, 508–522.

Kress, G. & Van Leeuwen, T. (2001). *Multimodal Discourse: The Modes and Media of Contemporary Communication*. London: Edward Arnold.

Laudon, K. C., & Laudon, J. P. (2004). *Management Information Systems: Managing the Digital Firm* (9th ed.). Upper Saddle River: Prentice Hall.

Liao, G., & Xia, D. (2023). Historical poem-quoting interaction: An interaction-speech act-ritual integrative study of fù in ancient China. *Journal of Pragmatics*, 214: 21–37.

Maamuujav, U., Olson, C. B., & Chung, H. (2021). Syntactic and lexical features of adolescent L2 students' academic writing. *Journal of Second Language Writing*, 53, 100822. https://doi.org/10.1016/j.jslw.2021.100822

Mandavilli, A. (2023, Aug., 10). Heat singes the mind, not just the body. *The New York Times*.

Meng, X. Y., et al. (2023). A versatile and tunable bio-patterning platform for the construction of various cell array biochips. *Biosensors and Bioelectronics*, 228, 115203. https://doi.org/10.1016/j.bios.2023.115203

Pavlou, V. (2020). Art technology integration: Digital storytelling as a transformative pedagogy in primary education. *International Journal of Art & Design Education*, 39: 195–210.

Pendry, P., Carr, A. M., Gee, N. R., & Vandagriff, J. L. (2020). Randomized trial examining effects of animal assisted intervention and stress related symptoms on college students' learning and study skills. *International Journal of Environmental Research and Public Health*, 17(6): 1909. https://doi.org/10.3390/ijerph17061909

Raccichini, R., Amores, M. & Hinds, G. (2019). Critical review of the use of reference electrodes in Li-Ion batteries: A diagnostic perspective. *Batteries*, 5(1): 12.

Bibliography

Rehm, C. D., et al. (2023). Trends and patterns of chickpea consumption among United States adults: Analyses of national health and nutrition examination survey data. *The Journal of Nutrition*, 153(5): 1567–1576.

Rehman, H. U., Hasan, A., & Reda, F. (2022). Challenges in reaching positive energy building level in apartment buildings in the Nordic climate: A techno-economic analysis. *Energy and Buildings*, 262, 111991. https://doi.org/10.1016/j.enbuild.2022.111991

Sandhya, M., & Prasad, M. (2017). Securing fingerprint templates using fused structures. *IET Biometrics*, 6(3): 173–182.

Sassine, A. J., Rabbitt, M. P., Jensen, A. C., Moshfegh, A. J., & Sahyoun, N. R. (2023). Development and validation of a physical food security tool for older adults. *The Journal of Nutrition*, *153*(4): 1273–1282.

Shafiq, S. I., Szczerbicki, E., & Sanín, C. (2019). Decisional DNA based intelligent knowledge model for flexible manufacturing system. *Journal of Intelligent & Fuzzy Systems*, *37*(6): 1–13.

Sun, S. Y., & Crosthwaite, P. (2022). Establish a niche via negation: A corpus-based study of negation within the move 2 sections of PhD thesis introductions. *Open Linguistics*, 8(1): 189–208.

Terrier, C., & Cohn, E. (2020). Boys lag behind: How teachers' gender biases affect student achievement. *Economics of Education Review*, 77, 101981. https://doi.org/10.1016/j.econedurev.2020.101981

Tiffany, G., et al. (2023). Generalizability of and lessons learned from a mixed-methods study conducted in three low- and middle-income countries to identify care pathways for atrial fibrillation. *Global Health Action*, 16(1), 2231763. https://doi.org/10.1080/16549716.2023.2231763

van den Berg, H. (2022). Animal languages in eighteenth-century German philosophy and science. *Studies in History and Philosophy of Science*, 93: 72–81.

Wang, K., et al. (2016). Vibration sensor approaches for the sand detection in gas-sand two phases flow. *Powder Technology*, *288*: 221–227.

Wang, S., Liu, G., & Wang, L. (2019). Crystal facet engineering of photoelectrodes for photoelectrochemical water splitting. *Chemical Reviews*, *119*(8): 5192–5247.

Willingham, E. (2023, June, 25). Teenagers skeptical of social media have a lower risk of eating disorders. *Scientific American*.

Wind, A. M. (2021). Nonlinearity and inter- and intra-individual variability in the extent of engagement in self-reflection and its role in second language writing: A multiple-case study. *System*, 103, 102672. https://doi.org/10.1016/j.system.2021.102672

Wu, P., et al. (2022). Comparative analysis of the texture, composition, antioxidant capacity and nutrients of natural gynogenesis blunt snout bream and its parent muscle. *Reproduction and Breeding*, 2(4): 149–155.

Xue, S., et al. (2023). Pollution prediction for heavy metals in soil-groundwater systems at smelting sites. *Chemical Engineering Journal*, 473, 145499. https://doi.org/10.1016/j.cej.2023.145499

Zhan, F., & Traugott, E. C. (2019). The development of the Chinese copula shì construction: A diachronic constructional perspective. *Functions of Language*, 26(2): 139–176.

Zhang, Y., Chang, R., Zuo, J., Shabunco, V., & Zheng, X. (2023). Regional disparity of residential solar panel diffusion in Australia: The roles of socio-economic factors. *Social Science Electronic Publishing*, 206, 808–819.

Zheng, X., et al. (2024). MAX-DOAS and in-situ measurements of aerosols and trace gases over Dongying, China: Insight into ozone formation sensitivity based on secondary HCHO. *Journal of Environmental Sciences*, 135, 656–668.

Zhong, R. Y., Xu, X., Klotz, E., & Newman, S. T. (2017). Intelligent manufacturing in the context of industry 4.0: A review. *Engineering, 3*(5): 616–630.

Zhu, D. (2021). Stress intensity factor and interaction analysis of offset parallel cracks in brittle solids. *European Journal of Mechanics—A/Solids*, 85, 104119. https://doi.org/10.1016/j.euromechsol.2020.104119

陈崇贤，李海薇，林晓玲，陈婉静，夏宇．（2023）．基于计算机视觉的夜间户外环境情绪感知特征研究．中国园林，39（2），20–25．

陈功，宫明玉．（2022）．多元反馈模式促进深度学习的行动研究．外语教学，43（3），60–66．

崔彤彤，姜洪涛．（2023）．虚拟旅游体验、真实性和满意度对实地旅游意向的影响研究——以敦煌莫高窟为例．地理与地理信息科学，39（3），122–129．

戴寅，王潇辰，郑雅妮，李振杰，洪俊丽．（2022）．分子印迹技术在生命科学研究中的进展．生物化工，8（3），159–161．

窦楠．（2021）．现代艺术设计中抽象艺术语言的应用．艺术品鉴，（35），81–83．

方超，黄斌．（2020）．学前教育对青少年成就发展的影响——基于CEPS数据的实证研究．教育学报，16（1），73–82．

何存花．（2001）．人力资源在资产负债表中的确认与计量．山西财经大学学报，（1），84–85．

冀玄玄，姜军松．（2023）．中国种植业面源污染的区域差异及其脱钩效应．中国农业资源与区划，（7），1–13．

李玲芳，陈占鹏，胡炎，邰能灵，高孟平，朱涛．（2021）．基于灵活性和经济性的可再生能源电力系统扩展规划．上海交通大学学报（哲学社会科学版），55（7），791–801．

李晓静，刘畅．（2023）．手机如何妨害青少年的睡眠？——基于全国数据的实证研究．中国青年研究，（7），26–33．

林成旭，甘浪，谭鑫平，李雪梅，闫旺，李倩，陈刚，廖广兰，刘智勇．（2023）．基于荧光原位杂交技术的全自动病理染色系统结构设计．中国机械工程，34（5），603–609．

刘博涵，赵璞，石智丹，刘明．（2019）．学术型研究生学术志趣的影响因素探析．研究生教育研究，（6），35–41．

Bibliography

刘清堂，李小娟，谢魁，常瑀倍，郑欣欣．（2022）．多模态学习分析实证研究的发展与展望．电化教育研究，43（1），71–78+85．

刘煦阳，段潮舒，蔡文生，邵学广．（2022）．可解释深度学习在光谱和医学影像分析中的应用．化学进展，34（12），2561–2572．

陆玄鸣，白敬，王保．（2023）．变刚度柔性夹持装置的研究进展．机电工程，40（11），1803–1813．

罗娜，王冬，王世芳，韩平．（2019）．太赫兹技术在农产品品质检测中的研究进展．光谱学与光谱分析，39（2），349–356．

马德刚，孟凡怡，林森，黄晓林．（2020）．间断供电对污泥电脱水效果的影响．天津大学学报（自然科学与工程技术版），53（3），284–290．

马前广．（2022）．大学生家庭功能与心理异常的关系：孤独感和性取向的作用．青少年犯罪问题，（6），15–27．

马强，戴军．（2023）．基于深度学习的跨社交网络用户匹配方法．电子与信息学报，45（7），2650–2658．

马忠法，孟爱华．（2013）．论我国《著作权法》立法宗旨的修改——以促进文化产业发展为视角．同济大学学报（社会科学版），24（3），103–109+116．

马忠新．（2022）．构建国内经济大循环制度影响因素的实证研究．统计与决策，38（24），89–92．

倪闽景．（2023）．从学习进化的视角看 ChatGPT/ 生成式人工智能对学习的影响．华东师范大学学报（教育科学版），41（7），151–161．

舒歌群，杨爽，王伟光，霍东兴，田华．（2022）．热再生氨基液流电池电堆模型建立及性能分析．天津大学学报（自然科学与工程技术版），55（12），1219–1229．

唐鹏，金炜东，张兴斌，张志军，邢铠鹏，霍志浩．（2021）．基于知识模型的接触网缺陷智能视觉辨识．控制与信息技术，（6），84–90．

王庆辉，赵凯航，宋国立，赵忆文，赵新刚．（2023）．基于增强现实的脊柱微创手术导航系统．机器人，（5），546–553．

王硕，李长波，许洪祝，赵国峥，梁慧，李东彧．（2023）．造纸废水活性污泥的微生物群落结构及多样性分析．微生物学杂志，43（3），19–29．

王伟清，王玲．显隐性教学和场风格对 EFL 学习者习得动词一般过去式的影响．外语研究，40（5），63–70．

王一博，郭鑫，刘智锋，王继民．（2023）．AI 生成与学者撰写中文论文摘要的检测与差异性比较研究——以图书馆学领域为例．情报杂志，42（9），127–134．

王毅，张宁，康重庆．（2015）．能源互联网中能量枢纽的优化规划与运行研究综述及展望．中国电机工程学报，35（22），5669–5681．

王幼琨．（2020）．大学生英语学习动机自我系统对动机调控策略的影响．外语教育研究前沿，3（1），53–61+88–89．

魏晖，吴晓文．（2023）．国际中文教育集成创新：内涵、价值和路径．世界汉语教学，37（2），147–156．

肖洋, 臧国全. (2023). 个人金融数据的敏感性识别与隐私计量研究. 情报理论与实践, 46 (9): 105–114+86.

徐光木, 熊旭辉, 张屹, 魏晴晴. (2023). ChatGPT 助推教育考试数字化转型：机遇、应用及挑战. 中国考试, (5), 19–28.

徐锦芬, 李霞. (2019). 社会文化理论视角下的高校英语教师学习研究. 现代外语, 42 (6), 842–854.

姚君喜. (2023). 外籍留学生汉语学习、媒介使用对中国文化认同的影响. 上海交通大学学报（哲学社会科学版）, 31 (6), 32–45.

岳芳, 顾新建, 郭剑锋, 曹玉华, 乐承毅. (2015). 概念知识地图协同创作过程中的群体决策模型. 科研管理, 36 (1), 127–134.

曾思慧. (2022). 基于循环经济视角的新能源汽车动力电池回收利用分析. 中国资源综合利用, 40 (12), 94–96.

张东, 田胜力, 肖德炎, 周剑敏. (2005). 相变储能材料技术及其在建筑节能中的应用. 上海建筑新技术研讨会论文集, 33–45.

张凯, 王九令, 李真珍, 胡婧, 王宁, 靳艳飞. (2022). 漫谈冰球大力击射中的力学原理. 力学与实践, 44 (2), 454–457.

张寅冬, 丁川. (2022). 基于政府补贴的创业投资定价与决策. 运筹与管理. http://kns.cnki.net/kcms/detail/34.1133.G3.20220801.1529.002.html.

赵世举, 程海燕. (2023). 术语命名理念与策略的更新刍议——以"元宇宙"为例. 语言文字应用, (1), 67–75.

郑咏滟, 李慧娴. (2023). 复杂动态系统理论视角下二语写作发展的变异性研究. 现代外语, 46 (5): 650–663.

种珊, 朱松丽. (2022). 我国塑料碳排放核算体系搭建与应用初探. 中国能源, 44 (12), 7–15.

周喜平. (2018). 关于计算机软件程序漏洞实时检测仿真. 计算机仿真, 35 (1), 247–250.

周晓. (2018). 多维互动模式对二语词汇习得的影响. 现代外语, 41 (5), 647–660.

周玮, 杨刚, 郑丹, 陈际焕, 陈晓东. (2023). 基于智能认知诊断性反馈的英语翻译学习研究. 现代教育技术, 33 (5), 70–78.

"清华社英语在线"（TUP English Online）平台使用指南

"清华社英语在线"集教、学、练、测、评、研等功能于一体，支持全媒体教学的泛在式外语学习。PC、移动端同步应用，提供互动式的教学环境、个性化的学习管理、多维度的学情监控、碎片化的应用场景，以实现混合式教学。平台致力于全方位提高教学效率、提升教学效果、优化学习体验，为高校英语教师和学生提供在线学习、交流、教学管理、测试评估等服务。

一、数字课程使用指南

Step 1：登录平台（PC 端、移动端均可）

PC 端：www.tsinghuaelt.com（推荐使用 360 或 Google Chrome 浏览器）；

移动端：微信内搜索小程序"清华社英语在线"或扫描下方小程序二维码。

Step 2：输入账号（登录账号、密码由平台创建）

（1）集体用户（学校教师统一授课）

由任课教师联系出版社，平台为学生统一创建登录账号。教师在平台开课后，学生进入教师课程学习。

（2）个人用户

登录界面点击【帮助中心】，联系平台在线客服获取账号密码，随后进入平台的公共课程内学习。

Step 3：激活课程（本书封底贴有教材配套验证码，输入以激活课程）

（1）进入教师课程后，点击【激活教材码】，刮开本书封底贴的激活码序列号并输入，即可激活课程开始学习；

（2）进入公共课程后，同上述方式激活课程后开始学习。

二、特别提示

1. 每本教材配套的激活码仅可在一个登录账号的配套课程中使用，激活成功后即失效，不可重复使用。
2. 数字课程的使用期限为一年，请在开学初仅输入需要学习的课程的激活码；如因过早输入非本学期所学课程的激活码，导致课程届时过期而无法使用，我社不负责补发激活码。
3. 激活码遗失不补，需联系教师或自行购买新的教材或激活码。

三、帮助中心

数字课程及平台使用的常见问题，请在登录界面或课程内的【帮助中心–常见问题】处点击查看；如有其他疑问，请咨询平台在线客服。